THE REMAINING TIME WE HAVE

HOW KNOWING LIFE'S MILESTONES TRANSFORMS OUR JOURNEY, REFLECTIONS ON LIVING FULLY THROUGH THE GIFT OF TIME, FINDING JOY AND MEANING IN LIFE'S MILESTONES TODAY, A STRESS-FREE GUIDE TO DISCOVERING MEANING IN LIFE

TAMER SALEH

CONTENTS

Introduction   11

1. FROM SCHOOL TO COLLEGE - THE
MAKING OF A PATH   15
A Journey in Self-Discovery   18
The Power of Choice and the Path Unseen   19
The Moral: Embracing Life's Lessons and
Moving Forward   20
Gratitude and a Look Forward   22

2. SHIFTING MY LIFE DIRECTION   27
Embracing the Challenges and Lessons of
Army Life   29
A Growing Restlessness   32
The Temptation of the Unknown   33
The Power of Risk: Fueling Growth and Self-
Discovery   38
A Leap into Freedom and Opportunity   39

3. THE GOLF LESSON THAT CHANGED
MY LIFE   45
Embracing Flexibility Over Force   48
Flexibility as a Virtue in Personal Growth   49
Flexibility in Career and Decision-Making   50
Flexibility as a Path to Resilience   51
Flexibility and Problem Solving   52
Flexibility and Letting Go of Perfectionism   53
Flexibility as a Guide to Living Fully   54
Real-Life Scenarios of "Letting Go"   54
Applying the Lesson Beyond the Golf Course   55
Learning the Value of Patience and Timing   56
Embracing the Unknown: The Benefits of a
Looser Grip on Life's Outcomes   57
The Power of Adjusting and Adapting   58

The Paradox of Control: Finding Freedom in Letting Go 58
Finding Joy in the Process Rather Than the Outcome 59
Developing Resilience Through Acceptance 60
The Influence of Flexibility on Creativity and Problem-Solving 60
Cultivating Inner Peace Through Letting Go 61

4. CROSSROADS IN MY LIFE 65
Rediscovering Values and Personal Alignment 72
Redefining Success and Achievement 73
The Art of Intentional Living 73
Learning to Savor Life's Simple Pleasures 74
Embracing the Power of Reflection and Growth 75
Finding Balance Between Giving and Receiving 76
Discovering the Joy of Personal Fulfillment 76
Embracing the Unknown with Open Arms 77
Building a Legacy Beyond Professional Success 78
The Shift from Professional Success to Personal Happiness 78
A Redefinition of Success 79
Letting Go of External Validation 80
Discovering Happiness in Relationships and Connections 81
The Role of Giving and Contribution 82
Embracing Simplicity and Contentment 83
Cultivating a Life of Purpose and Fulfillment 83
Happiness as the Foundation of a Meaningful Legacy 84
The Joy of Creating Lasting Memories 85
The Legacy of Kindness and Generosity 86
Contribution to Community: A Lasting Impact 86
Remembering What Truly Matters 87
Conclusion: Crafting a Legacy of Joy and Meaning 89
A New Path Forward 89

5. THE LAST CHAPTER IN LIFE . . . 91
The Fleeting Nature of Time . . . 91
The Impact of Time Awareness . . . 92
The Psychology of Time and Fulfillment . . . 93
The Challenge of Living Fully in the Moment . . . 94
A Life of Continuous Presence and Purpose . . . 95
Embracing the Impermanence of Time . . . 96
The Illusion of "Someday" . . . 96
The Endless Cycle of Postponement . . . 97
The Assumptions of the X and Y Dates . . . 98
Living Fully Without Waiting . . . 99
The Role of the Chronopath in Breaking the Cycle . . . 100
Reclaiming Life's Simple Pleasures . . . 100
Embracing a Mindset of Presence and Purpose . . . 101
When Life Forces Us to Stop . . . 102
The Concept of X and Y Dates . . . 103
Lessons from the Unforeseen . . . 104
Embracing the Y Date as Motivation . . . 105
Redefining Purpose Through the Y Date . . . 105
The Y Date as a Catalyst for Gratitude . . . 106
Transforming Fear of Mortality into Purpose . . . 107
How the Y Date Guides Daily Choices . . . 108
Embracing a Life Without the Illusion of Forever . . . 108
Living Each Day with a Sense of Completion . . . 109
Conclusion: The Y Date as a Pathway to Authenticity . . . 110
Finding My Purpose . . . 110
Living with the Chronopath Mindset . . . 111
Lessons for the Future . . . 111

Final Conclusion: Embracing the Journey as It Is . . . 115
References . . . 123

BOOK DESCRIPTION

Imagine a watch that reveals your future milestones—when you'll find love, encounter challenges, and even glimpse the end of your life's journey. Would you live differently?

This memoir explores the power of reflection, resilience, and gratitude. Through vivid chapters on pivotal moments from a challenging childhood, demanding military service, and an intense corporate career, the author shares lessons learned about perseverance, the importance of flexibility, and the strength of embracing life's unpredictable nature. He introduces The Chronopath, a fictional watch that symbolizes life's milestones, encouraging readers to confront time's fleeting nature and to re-evaluate priorities before it's too late. With each chapter, readers are invited to ask themselves: What would you do if you knew your time was limited?

As the author journeys through life's crossroads, he discovers that true success is found not just in professional achievements but in meaningful relationships, personal growth, and a life lived with purpose. This story will inspire readers to reflect on their own paths and find gratitude in every moment, knowing that each choice, challenge, and success shapes a legacy worth leaving.

OUTLINE

INTRODUCTION

- Introduces the concept of *The Chronopath*, a metaphorical watch that prompts readers to reflect on life's fleeting moments. It sets up the themes of self-reflection, purpose, and gratitude that will guide the journey.

CHAPTER 1: FROM SCHOOL TO COLLEGE – THE MAKING OF A PATH

- **Theme:** Resilience and Adaptability
- Details the author's early years, navigating a strict Catholic education and difficult family dynamics, fostering a deep sense of resilience.
- Reflects on choosing a challenging path by joining a military engineering college, highlighting the value of hard decisions and the foundation they lay for future success.

CHAPTER 2: SHIFTING MY LIFE DIRECTION

- **Theme:** The Power of Risk and Embracing the Unknown

- Covers his years in the military, where rigorous discipline and leadership skills were forged.
- Faced with a choice between stability in the army and the uncertainty of the corporate world, the author chooses risk and growth over predictability.
- The lesson: Growth often requires stepping into the unknown.

CHAPTER 3: THE GOLF LESSON THAT CHANGED MY LIFE

- **Theme:** Flexibility and Letting Go of Control
- A pivotal golf lesson teaches the importance of adaptability and release, showing that force is not always necessary for success.
- Applies the lesson to life, emphasizing that sometimes "letting go" leads to better results and less stress.

CHAPTER 4: CROSSROADS IN MY LIFE

- **Theme:** The Impact of Time and the Cost of Delayed Fulfillment
- Reflects on reaching a point where career goals no longer satisfy, prompting a re-evaluation of life's priorities.
- Discusses the relentless demands of the corporate world and the sacrifices made, encouraging readers to assess their own time use and consider what truly brings fulfillment.

CHAPTER 5: THE FINAL CHAPTER IN LIFE

- **Theme:** Purpose and the Role of Gratitude
- Reflects on the inevitability of life's end, symbolized by the "Y Date."
- Discusses the importance of aligning life with personal values, finding meaning in the present, and preparing a legacy of love, growth, and gratitude.
- Emphasizes that understanding one's purpose is key to a fulfilled life, and encourages readers to live intentionally.

FINAL CONCLUSION: EMBRACING THE JOURNEY AS IT IS

- Recaps key lessons from each chapter, urging readers to embrace gratitude, live authentically, and trust in their journey.
- Encourages readers to use each choice and challenge as a stepping stone to a fulfilling life, understanding that their legacy lies in the love they share, the lives they touch, and the gratitude they carry forward.

INTRODUCTION

Have you ever wondered what it would be like to know the significant milestones of your life before they happen? Imagine a watch that tells you not only when you'll find love, achieve success, or face struggles but also reveals the final chapter of your journey. Would knowing these events change the way you live today? Would it inspire you to approach each day with a new perspective? If you knew when your story would end, would you make different choices, focus on other goals, or simply learn to let go and enjoy each moment?

As we live, we often get so wrapped up in our routines, goals, and daily struggles that we forget to pause and ask, "Am I truly living for myself?" I know this because I've been there. At 56, after dedicating decades to my career as an engineer, I found myself caught in the relentless cycle of long workdays, endless meetings, and the constant push for success. The demands were never-ending, and as much as I tried to balance family, career, and personal growth, I sometimes wondered: where in all this was *I*?

For over 30 years, I pushed forward, believing that the sacrifices were worth it and that each goal achieved would bring fulfillment. But as I moved from one role to another, achieving success and reaching milestones, I began to feel a growing need for something different. Early this year, that realization came to a head. For the first time, I felt drained—not just physically but emotionally and mentally drained. The thought of continuing on autopilot, constantly chasing one achievement after another, felt empty. I had to ask myself: Is this truly the life I want? Would I continue this way if I knew how much time I had left?

In this state of reflection, I began to imagine a tool—a watch of sorts—that could show me where my life was headed. This idea, which I call *The Chronopath*, became a way for me to explore what it would mean to know my future milestones, to understand not only the end but each step that would bring me closer to it. How might my life have changed if I'd known in advance the moments that would matter most? What if, in my younger years, I'd had a glimpse of the person I'd become, the choices I'd make, and the paths I would leave behind?

With *The Chronopath* in mind, I took a journey back through my life, looking at each significant milestone with fresh eyes. I asked myself, "If I had known then what I know now, would I have done things differently? Would I have made more time for myself or focused less on the rush to achieve?" More importantly, I considered the impact of each decision on the person I am today. By revisiting these moments, I began to see that each step, each hard choice, and each joyful moment led me precisely to where I needed to be.

Through this reflection, I discovered the true power of gratitude. It wasn't only about appreciating the good times but about understanding that every experience—the struggles and the successes—played a role in shaping my life. I saw that every decision, whether suitable or challenging, contributed to my growth and journey. *The Chronopath* became less about knowing what was to come and more about accepting what had been. Looking back, I realized that the life I'd built, with all its ups and downs, was worth every moment, and I wouldn't change a thing.

In this book, I invite you to join me as I revisit each of these pivotal moments, imagining how *The Chronopath* might have influenced my choices and reshaped my path. Through each chapter, I'll share my reflections on milestones in my career, relationships, and personal growth. More than that, I hope to inspire you to think about your own journey. Life is full of unknowns, and it's easy to worry about what's around the corner. But if there's one thing I've learned, it's that sometimes the best thing we can do is to embrace the uncertainty, trust in the process, and approach each day with gratitude.

In the end, life is about the moments we live, not the moments we anticipate. It's about learning to find joy in the present, appreciate where we are, and trust that each decision will lead us closer to the life we are meant to live. As I share my journey with you, I hope you'll find inspiration in my story and the courage to embrace your own.

1

FROM SCHOOL TO COLLEGE - THE MAKING OF A PATH

Growing up, I was born into a world that would test me in ways I could never have anticipated. I came into this life in 1968, raised in a household that was fractured early on. My parents divorced when I was just five, and in an unusual split, I stayed with my father while my sister lived with my mother. This division of family alone was complex enough for a child, but life with my father brought its own set of challenges. He remarried, and I quickly discovered that my stepmother was less than kind. Her treatment was unfair and often harsh, leaving me with a sense of isolation and lack that would haunt me through childhood and beyond.

As I navigated those formative years, I went to a strict French Catholic school, an institution that seemed to mirror the rigidity of my home life. This school, led by stern church priests, had little tolerance for excuses or mistakes. Discipline was the foundation upon which our education was built, and we were constantly reminded that life's best decisions were often the hardest. "Choose the difficult path," one priest would frequently say, "for it will teach you more than you can imagine." At first, this didn't make much sense to me. Why, when life was hard enough, should I make it harder? Yet those words stuck with me.

In hindsight, I realize now how much that schooling shaped me despite the strict and often cold environment. I learned lessons not only in academics but in discipline, resilience, and the value of hard work. This foundation would later give me the strength to overcome some of my life's greatest challenges. But back then, I was simply a boy trying to survive. I faced constant comparisons to my classmates, many of whom lived in more privileged circumstances. They had access to things that were out of reach for me, from nice clothes to simple treats. Financially, we were far from wealthy—perhaps just above the line of struggling, yet without the comforts others took for granted.

When the school organized a class trip to a nearby city, I knew joining them was out of the question. The cost was beyond what my father could afford, so I created excuses. I'd tell friends my parents were taking me to our nonexistent family cottage, all to save face. The little joys and experiences others around me had were reminders of what I lacked. While my friends talked excitedly about their plans, I worked hard to mask my disappointment.

The struggles at school were compounded by the atmosphere at home. My father and stepmother's relationship was fraught with tension, and their arguments filled our house with a constant sense of unease. It became challenging to focus on my studies, even as my workload grew, spread across three languages—Arabic, French, and English. Every day seemed to bring fresh academic and emotional challenges, but I resolved to push through. I reminded myself of my teacher's words: "The difficult path is worth taking."

By 1986, I had completed my high school education, which felt monumental given everything I had endured. Against the odds, I graduated with a grade that enabled me to pursue further studies at a respected university. But as I looked at my future options, I felt a strange conflict. To stay at the local university meant continuing to live with my father and step-mother, and I was ready for a change, a challenge that would break me free of the limitations of my current life.

A second option, a more grueling path, caught my attention: the military college of engineering. In my country, only those with brothers were required to complete military service, but as an only child, I was exempt. Volunteering to join the army was unconventional, even unthinkable for many young men, as it meant facing an environment known for its rigorous training, strict discipline, and endless rules.

I recalled my teacher's advice once again. Could choosing this more difficult route really offer something worthwhile? It was not the "smart" choice by conventional standards, and people around me questioned my reasoning. But deep down, I sensed that I needed a drastic shift. I decided to commit to the military college, accepting that life would become even more challenging. I was prepared to step into an experience that would demand far more of me than I had yet faced.

A JOURNEY IN SELF-DISCOVERY

As I entered military college, my life transformed in unexpected ways. Over the next five years, I lived and breathed the dual worlds of military training and engineering. I learned about technical principles by day and underwent physical drills and discipline exercises by night. Every moment demanded focus, resilience, and endurance. Surprisingly, it felt more manageable than I'd expected—perhaps because of the toughness I had developed over the years.

The military environment, harsh as it was, gave me something invaluable: a sense of structure, purpose, and personal responsibility. My personality underwent a dramatic change. From someone who had struggled to find his footing, I evolved into a young man with direction and resilience. I began to see obstacles as part of the journey, each teaching me to persevere, focus, and make the best of challenging circumstances.

My civilian peers would have had a very different experience, likely filled with the freedoms and social scenes of a typical university student. But I felt I had gained something far more lasting. The discipline I was absorbing was becoming a defining part of me, teaching me that life's challenges are not always something to escape but often an opportunity to grow.

THE POWER OF CHOICE AND THE PATH UNSEEN

Reflecting on those years, I realize that choosing the harder path brought invaluable experiences. I imagine if I had been wearing the *Chronopath*—the watch that could reveal my future—during that time. It would have shown me the version of my life that lay down each path: the comfort and ease of a civil university on the one hand and the arduous but enriching military college experience on the other. And yet, even with the insight of *The Chronopath*, I'm confident I would have chosen exactly as I did.

Had I opted for the university route, my life today would have looked completely different. I may have missed out on the lessons that only adversity can teach. I might not have gained the resilience, self-confidence, or drive that now define me. Looking back, I feel that the choice I made was truly the best one, as it shaped me into a person capable of handling life's challenges with patience, strength, and gratitude.

THE MORAL: EMBRACING LIFE'S LESSONS AND MOVING FORWARD

This chapter of my life taught me a valuable truth: that our choices, especially the difficult ones, shape us far more than the easy victories ever could. Looking back, I see that every tough decision, every hard-won lesson, and every moment of struggle became a building block of who I am today. When faced with life's crossroads, it's tempting to choose the easiest or most convenient path. Yet, if I had avoided the hard choices, I would have missed the opportunity to cultivate resilience and strength in ways I could never have anticipated.

One of the most transformative aspects of making difficult decisions is the perspective it brings. Life isn't always going to be smooth or forgiving, and our ability to face adversity is often what determines our success, happiness, and growth. The military experience, as tough as it was, gifted me this understanding. It taught me that setbacks are not a reason to give up; they are the very fuel that drives us forward. Every day in that challenging environment, I learned to push myself beyond what I thought were my limits. I realized that obstacles, though frustrating in the moment, are often the very things that shape our character.

This understanding became a foundation for how I approached other aspects of life. By the time I completed my military service, I could see that the choices I made had honed my focus on what was genuinely important to me. I learned not to be distracted by minor frustrations or superficial desires. This focus helped me zero in on my goals, turning my energy and resources toward things that would enrich my life rather than complicate it. When you go through hardship, you begin to differentiate between what's truly meaningful and what takes up space. You see, life's big decisions require us to prioritize our long-term goals over temporary discomfort.

Thinking back to my younger self, I wish I could tell him how important it is to find meaning in the journey, not just in the destination. Life is not simply a series of events; it's a rich tapestry of experiences that demand our appreciation. It's easy to get lost in thoughts of "what could be" or "what should be." But when we let ourselves truly experience the journey—its hardships, triumphs, and daily grind—we start to understand that meaning isn't something we find at the end. We create meaning through the lessons we learn and the resilience we cultivate along the way.

I think of life as a river, constantly flowing, sometimes calm and sometimes turbulent. In this river, it's easy to focus on getting to the next bend, the next smooth stretch. Yet it's in those turbulent stretches that we discover our strength, learn new skills, and find our resilience. It's these parts of the journey that truly shape us. Embracing this mindset, where we view challenges as growth opportunities, helps us find a sense of fulfillment. Instead of feeling anxious about the future or regretful about the past, we can learn to be present, to value each lesson, and to trust that every challenge has something to teach us. Life becomes not a series of struggles to endure but a journey to savor.

Learning to appreciate every part of the journey, especially the problematic parts, gives us a sense of purpose that goes beyond personal gain. It allows us to cultivate a mindset that seeks meaning in every experience. This lesson taught me to stop fighting against the current and instead navigate it gracefully. I learned that every hardship, every choice, every uncomfortable moment was building a more capable and resilient version of myself. By embracing this journey with all its twists and turns, I've come to value the person I've become—a person shaped by experiences rather than a perfect, unhindered path.

GRATITUDE AND A LOOK FORWARD

As I reflect on these years, I find myself deeply grateful for the journey I have traveled. Looking back, the hard road gave me not only growth but a profound understanding of what it means to live truly. Choosing to accept challenges rather than avoid them helped me uncover my values and taught me to appreciate every step along the way. I have come to realize that gratitude is not only an appreciation for the good moments but also a deep respect for the difficult ones that shape us.

Gratitude shifts our perspective. When we practice gratitude, we're not just acknowledging the good things we have but also recognizing the experiences that have taught us resilience, patience, and understanding. There's immense value in appreciating not just what we've achieved but the journey that brought us there. When I reflect on the tough decisions I made, like choosing military college over a traditional path, I feel an overwhelming sense of thankfulness. That choice taught me far more than academic lessons; it taught me the value of perseverance, discipline, and self-reliance.

What's powerful about gratitude is that it helps us see the hidden gifts within our challenges. It's easy to feel grateful when things go well, but when we can look at difficult experiences with appreciation, we open ourselves up to a fuller understanding of life. Gratitude isn't about pretending everything is perfect. Instead, it's about recognizing that even in our struggles, valuable lessons can be learned. By embracing gratitude, we learn to look beyond our circumstances and appreciate the growth they inspire in us. This mindset allows us to see the beauty in the journey itself, even when the path is rocky.

Reflecting on these experiences has shown me that true strength comes from accepting life's ups and downs. It's a reminder that we are shaped by every choice we make, every hardship we endure, and every lesson we learn. As we move forward, gratitude can serve as our compass, helping us to navigate life's challenges with a sense of purpose and peace. This mindset has changed how I approach my future. Instead of fearing the unknown, I welcome it, knowing that whatever comes my way, I have the resilience to face it. Gratitude gives us the courage to face life's uncertainties with an open heart and a clear mind.

In embracing gratitude, we find a way to honor our journey, to see our life for what it truly is—a series of experiences that build us, challenge us, and ultimately shape us. This journey of reflecting on my past, of examining the choices I made and the paths I took, isn't just a personal story. It's a reminder for anyone standing at their own crossroads: Don't fear the hard path. Choose it. The most rewarding truths are often found in the places we least expect. The struggles we face are the very elements that make life meaningful, rich, and worthwhile.

So, as I look to the future, I'm filled with a sense of peace. I don't need to know what's around every corner. I've come to trust that each moment, each decision, will bring with it the lessons I need. And while I can't predict every outcome, I know that with gratitude as my guide, I'll face whatever comes my way with an open mind and an open heart. Life is a journey meant to be embraced, cherished, and appreciated for all its ups and downs. Embracing this truth allows us to see the beauty in both our struggles and our triumphs.

As I move forward, I carry with me a commitment to honor every part of my journey, to approach each new challenge with gratitude, and to see each day as an opportunity to learn, grow, and give back. For anyone reading this, I hope that my story serves as a reminder to look at life through the lens of gratitude and courage. It's a mindset that allows us to see that no matter how challenging the road, there is always a lesson waiting, always an opportunity to become a better version of ourselves. And when we view life this way, we find a deeper appreciation for the journey itself, knowing that every experience, good or bad, has a purpose.

Embracing the lessons of our past and welcoming the possibilities of our future with gratitude is, in the end, one of life's greatest achievements. It is through this lens that we can find peace in the present moment, and it's through this practice that we learn to live fully, appreciate deeply, and face the future with open arms.

2

SHIFTING MY LIFE DIRECTION

It's 1996, and I find myself at a pivotal point in my life. After five intense years of service as an officer engineer, I've reached the peak of my current role within the army. My time in the military has shaped me in ways I could never have anticipated. Looking back on the last ten years—five spent training and five in service—I realize how transformative they've been. From enduring the relentless heat and isolation of the desert to commanding in the city's high-stakes environment, army life has added countless layers to my character. These experiences equipped me with an unshakeable sense of discipline, a persistent sense of responsibility, and the ability to perform under pressure.

The army was not just a career but a profound, almost brutal education in the power of persistence, precision, and adaptability. This period of my life taught me to focus amidst chaos, solve complex issues under tight deadlines, and push through insurmountable challenges. The stakes were often high; there was no room for error, and yet, time after time, I found myself achieving what had seemed impossible just moments before.

However, as I advanced in rank, a growing sense of restlessness began to surface. Although my career in the army was secure, with a predictable path of promotions and responsibilities, I felt like I was no longer learning. The path ahead was clear but stagnant, well-trodden yet uninspiring. The prospect of remaining in the military, while stable, felt suffocating. My passion for engineering and innovation seemed stifled, and I began to crave a new challenge. My mind kept wandering to the uncharted territories of the corporate world, a world that promised growth but also uncertainty and risk.

EMBRACING THE CHALLENGES AND LESSONS OF ARMY LIFE

The years I spent in the army were defined by unrelenting challenges, each one testing and ultimately fortifying me in ways that few other experiences could. My time stationed in the desert, far removed from the comforts of city life, was an initiation into a world of relentless endurance and mental fortitude. The heat was oppressive, unyielding, and exhausting; the isolation cut through even the strongest resolve. Every day felt like a new test, not just of my physical abilities but also of my inner strength and determination. It was there, amidst the vast sandscapes and limited resources, that I learned to stand on my own, relying solely on my wits and willpower. I discovered a hidden well of resilience, drawing strength from moments of solitude and finding clarity in making decisions with unwavering precision.

This time in the desert demanded that I develop survival instincts and adaptability—qualities I had unknowingly cultivated since childhood. Dealing with my father and the complexities of that relationship had instilled in me a unique resilience. I had learned to adapt, maneuver around situations beyond my control, and find ways to assert my sense of self without directly opposing authority. I realized that these coping mechanisms, once necessary for self-preservation, had become an invaluable skill set in the harsh military environment. My ability to read situations and strategize ways to handle challenging dynamics, rooted in my early years, became my compass during those demanding desert days.

When I moved into city operations and took on a higher rank, the nature of the challenges shifted but didn't ease. While the environment was less physically extreme, the structure and pressures of my new role brought a different kind of test. Leading people in a more complex, politically charged setting requires patience, empathy, and a strategic approach to human interaction. My unit was a mosaic of individuals from various educational and social backgrounds. Some soldiers struggled with basic literacy alongside officers with distinct training and mindsets, each carrying their unique strengths and weaknesses. Leading in this environment required an intense understanding of human behavior, something I had begun developing from my childhood interactions with my father.

Navigating these differences required a skill that was both strategic and intuitive. Much like in my younger years, I had to balance authority with empathy, commanding respect while remaining approachable and understanding. This delicate balancing act helped me connect with my unit on a deeper level, instilling trust and respect. I learned to communicate in ways that each person would understand and respond to, whether by adapting my approach or simplifying complex instructions. Just as I had maneuvered around complex family dynamics, I now found myself navigating the military hierarchy with a refined sense of diplomacy and adaptability.

In the military, there was no sidestepping responsibility. Every task was not just a job but an order, a mission with real and immediate consequences. The stakes were incredibly high, and failure wasn't an option. Time and again, I found myself in situations where decisions had to be made quickly and decisively under enormous pressure, driven by the knowledge that the lives of my team depended on me. There was no room for error, and each experience sharpened my ability to think on my feet, even when the pressure felt overwhelming. I became adept at thriving under stress, a skill that would later prove invaluable in my corporate career, where the stakes, though different, were equally high.

Reflecting on this period, I realized how deeply the army's discipline had seeped into my bones. It had molded me into a person who took full accountability for my actions, always understanding that each decision and command came with a ripple effect. Learning to manage my time effectively, orchestrate plans with precision, and handle challenging situations with calmness and focus became second nature. These were not just skills for professional use; they were tools that extended into my personal life, helping me navigate relationships and complex situations with a calm, disciplined approach. The sense of responsibility and resilience instilled in me by the army has been a guiding force in my life ever since.

The military was, in many ways, a crucible. It pushed me to the edges of my limits, shaping and refining my character. Every high-pressure situation was an opportunity to learn, to test my resolve, and to build the capacity to handle even more significant challenges in the future. It was within this environment that I truly came to value the lessons I had learned from my past. I began to appreciate how my early experiences with my father had gifted me an understanding of adaptability, resourcefulness, and resilience. These weren't just survival skills but essential qualities that allowed me to lead, inspire, and endure under some of the most demanding conditions.

The qualities I earned through my family and military experiences became my foundation. They helped me navigate the army's unique pressures and later provided me with a solid footing in the corporate world, where the rules were different but the challenges no less daunting. I understood, on a deep level, that I could adapt no matter how difficult the situation. I could assess, maneuver, and ultimately find a way through. The military taught me discipline, but my early life taught me adaptability, and together, these qualities became the key to my success. I had been shaped by both, prepared to face life's challenges head-on, with a mindset that embraced resilience, discipline, and an unwavering commitment to moving forward.

A GROWING RESTLESSNESS

Yet, as each year passed, I felt an unshakeable sense of restlessness begin to creep in. The comfort of the familiar had started to feel restrictive. I was skilled at my job and proficient in managing the demands of army life, but I could see a clear and predictable future stretching before me. Promotions and responsibilities would follow steadily, leading to an eventual retirement with a solid pension. This security was enticing, but at what cost? I felt my curiosity, my passion for engineering, and my desire to keep learning were slowly being smothered. I wasn't growing. I wasn't evolving.

The military was stable, structured, and guaranteed. There was little risk, and by all traditional measures, my career was set. But I began to wonder if stability was truly what I wanted. The army path promised a respectable career, yet I couldn't escape the thought that staying would lead to a slow erosion of my spirit. I had reached a point where my role was more about leadership and administration than about the engineering and problem-solving that initially drew me to this path. I feared that I would become stagnant, confined within a framework that no longer challenged me.

THE TEMPTATION OF THE UNKNOWN

As my desire for change grew stronger, I found myself drawn toward the idea of leaving the army—a notion that was as thrilling as it was daunting. I had spent years in an environment that provided structure, stability, and a clearly defined path, a place where promotions were almost predictable and advancement followed a prescribed course. But there was something powerful in the idea of stepping into the unknown, of shaking off the predictability of military life and leaping into a world without guarantees. I knew the corporate world would present new challenges, new industries, and the chance to work with technology that lay outside the purview of military frameworks. The potential to once again feel the thrill of learning and adapting ignited a spark within me, reminding me of the exhilaration that comes with taking on the unfamiliar.

The decision to leave the military, however, was not one I took lightly. The army had given me so much—a sense of purpose, valuable skills, and a place where I had repeatedly proven myself. But as I weighed the prospects, I couldn't ignore a growing sense of stagnation. In the military, my path was all but set. I could look ahead and see the promotions lined up, each one carrying new responsibilities but not necessarily new challenges. I would rise in rank, but the career trajectory was limited, and my growth as an engineer would be restrained, becoming more administrative than technical with each promotion.

It was at this crossroads that I began envisioning the role of my Chronopath, a fictional watch that reveals the unfolding paths of our future—if I continued in the army or if I chose to leave. The Chronopath allowed me to imagine the two possible lives I might lead. On the one hand, staying meant a life of stability, predictability, and comfort—a road I could walk with my eyes closed. But the more I glimpsed down this path, the more I felt a sense of inevitable mental decline, a life in which my curiosity and desire for challenge would slowly die. The monotony of routine might offer a secure retirement, but it would drain me of the hunger to learn and the passion to grow.

On the other hand, the Chronopath showed me the winding and uncertain road that came with leaving the army. I saw a path marked by unknowns and risks, a journey filled with twists and turns where I would be forced to reinvent myself over and over. I could almost feel the weight of the challenges I would face, the obstacles that would require me to call upon every ounce of resilience I had cultivated. But I also saw potential—a vision of boundless growth, of travel, and of immersing myself in new industries and learning opportunities. While uncertain, I saw a future that would allow me to expand beyond the constraints of my military identity and unlock a world of possibilities.

The Chronopath's vision was an invitation to imagine the life that could be, should I choose to take the leap. This fictional watch revealed the stakes of the choice before me: to stay and live a life of relative ease or to step into a future of uncharted possibilities. The more I thought about it, the more I realized I could either cling to the comfort of the known or embrace the transformative power of risk. In many ways, it felt as though I were standing at the edge of a cliff, gazing out at the vast expanse of what might be, knowing that there was no turning back once I leaped. The unknown was both a beacon and a challenge, drawing me forward with the promise of freedom, growth, and the ability to shape my own destiny.

Leaving the military would mean more than just a career change; it would mean relinquishing the predictability that had defined my life for over a decade. I would be stepping into an environment governed by unwritten rules, where every interaction, project, and position demanded adaptability and ingenuity. In the corporate world, I'd be surrounded by unfamiliar dynamics—office politics, organizational hierarchies, and different professional etiquettes. These things were foreign to me, but the thought of learning to navigate them awakened an inner drive I hadn't felt in years.

The risk of failure was real, and the potential for missteps was high, but so was the opportunity for self-discovery and growth. The corporate world would push me to apply the discipline, leadership, and crisis-management skills I had developed in the military to entirely new arenas. I would no longer have the clear guidance of military protocols or the unyielding support of a structured chain of command. Instead, I would be on my own, relying on my resourcefulness and my determination to prove myself in a civilian setting.

Ultimately, I realized that this leap wasn't just about pursuing a new career—it was about reclaiming my freedom and reigniting my passion for learning and self-improvement. The decision felt like a return to my younger self, that version of me who had always been willing to push boundaries and face challenges head-on. In choosing the unknown, I was choosing a life where I would never stop evolving, where every setback would be a lesson, and every success a stepping stone to something greater.

The Chronopath's alternate vision of my life in the military served as a powerful reminder of what I stood to gain by leaving. While I would have continued to rise in rank and earn respect, the very nature of my growth would have been confined to the boundaries of my military role. I would have watched the years pass by, each promotion bringing me a little closer to retirement but a little farther from the dreams I'd once held. The Chronopath showed me that staying would mean sacrificing my curiosity, my hunger for challenge, and, ultimately, a part of myself that longed for change.

The decision to leave was a testament to my willingness to embrace life's uncertainties. Accepting risk as a companion on my journey was a conscious choice. By choosing the unpredictable path, I accepted that growth is often uncomfortable and that true fulfillment rarely comes from playing it safe. In taking this leap, I committed to living boldly, facing the unknown with open arms, and trusting in my ability to navigate whatever challenges lay ahead.

At that moment, standing at the edge of my decision, I felt the fear of the unknown dissolves into excitement. The Chronopath had shown me both paths and now the choice was mine. I understood that stepping into the unknown was not just a career move—it was a declaration of independence, a commitment to a life of continuous learning and growth. The corporate world, with all its risks and uncertainties, became my new frontier, a place where I could build a future defined by courage, resilience, and a willingness to embrace every opportunity.

And so, I chose to jump. I left the army and began my journey into civilian life, fully aware that there would be challenges and setbacks. But the decision was made with clarity, grounded in the knowledge that the life I wanted could only be found on the other side of risk. In choosing this path, I was accepting a life of limitless possibilities—a future where I would always have something new to learn, something new to strive for, and the freedom to chart my own course.

THE POWER OF RISK: FUELING GROWTH AND SELF-DISCOVERY

I realized that true growth often requires us to take risks and abandon what is comfortable and secure in favor of something uncertain. Risk is not just a peril; it's a catalyst for transformation. It's in these moments of vulnerability, when we have no guarantees, that we uncover the depths of our resilience and determination. Leaving the military wasn't just a career decision; it was a decision to take control of my life, to choose growth over stagnation, and to embrace the difficulties that comes with stepping into the unknown.

Taking this leap was like plunging into the deep ocean, not knowing what I would find beneath the surface. But that very uncertainty brought a sense of aliveness I hadn't felt in years. I was eager to learn, to test myself, and to prove that I could adapt to any situation. The risks were real, but so was the potential for a richer, more fulfilling life. I knew that by taking this step, I was choosing a path that would challenge me in ways I couldn't yet imagine. And it was in that challenge that I saw the potential to become a better, stronger version of myself.

In the end, I decided to leave the army. It was the hardest decision I had ever made, but it was also the most liberating. For the first time in a decade, I was stepping out of the rigid confines of military life and into a world of possibilities. I didn't know what lay ahead, but I was ready to face it head-on, armed with the skills, discipline, and resilience that the army had instilled in me.

A LEAP INTO FREEDOM AND OPPORTUNITY

Transitioning to civilian life was far from easy; it was a shock to the system in every sense. After a decade spent within the defined structure, discipline, and chain of command that characterized my military experience, I now found myself in uncharted territory. The world beyond the army operated by a different set of rules, filled with nuances I hadn't been exposed to before. I had to reorient myself, redefining who I was outside the military framework and discovering what it meant to navigate the complexities of civilian life. This transition required adapting to a new culture, where success wasn't defined by rank, uniform, or a clear mission but by my ability to innovate, communicate, and connect with others in ways I hadn't practiced before.

At first, every interaction and task felt like a challenge. Gone were the predictable procedures of the military; instead, I found myself in an environment where ambiguity was typical, where directives weren't always given explicitly, and where I had to piece together solutions using different skills. I was forced to think outside the box, to adapt quickly, and to rely on my intuition and personal judgment. I had to recalibrate my approach to leadership and communication, no longer depending on hierarchy but on persuasion, influence, and collaboration.

Despite the initial difficulty, this new freedom to chart my course was exhilarating. I was no longer confined to a single path or role; instead, I had the autonomy to make choices that resonated with my passions and values. The challenges I faced weren't simply obstacles; they became tests of my resilience and adaptability, stretching my abilities and helping me grow in ways I never anticipated. In the corporate world, the rules of engagement were unspoken, constantly shifting, and required a level of flexibility that the military couldn't fully prepare me for. But with each hurdle, I felt a profound sense of growth and achievement.

The corporate world, unpredictable as it was, turned out to be a place rich with innovation, creativity, and constant learning. The pace was quick, the stakes high, but each day offered me a new opportunity to push myself beyond my comfort zone. I was faced with scenarios that required me to build upon the strengths I had developed in the military while also developing new ones. I began to see that success in this world was less about following orders and more about adaptability, quick thinking, and creative problem-solving. It was a world that rewarded risk-taking and celebrated individuality.

Leaving the army was the best decision I could have made. This leap of faith required courage, resilience, and a willingness to face the unknown. By taking this risk, I opened the door to a life filled with growth, adventure, and self-discovery. It was a decision to face uncertainty head-on, knowing full well that the outcomes were far from guaranteed. But with each challenge came a new layer of resilience, a new lesson learned, and a deeper understanding of who I was and what I was capable of achieving.

Reflecting on this journey, I see now that each challenge, each setback, was a stepping stone. Every problematic moment pushed me closer to my goal of self-discovery and growth. It would have been easy to stay in the comfort of the military and follow the pre-determined steps laid out for me.

Yet, by choosing the riskier path, I allowed myself to learn, evolve, and thrive in ways that wouldn't have been possible if I had stayed within my comfort zone. The decision to step away from the predictable path of the military was ultimately a decision to fully embrace life, with all its messiness, complexity, and beauty.

One of the most valuable lessons I learned from this leap was the importance of perseverance. There were times in this new journey when I doubted myself, where the weight of uncertainty felt almost unbearable. The corporate world was less forgiving in some ways; there was no clear-cut structure to fall back on, no rank or insignia to distinguish one's place.

But perseverance taught me to keep pushing and to stay committed to my vision, even when the going got tough. In the military, perseverance meant pushing through physical and mental limits. In the civilian world, it was more about grit, resilience, and the courage to keep going despite the fear of failure.

And through it all, gratitude became a grounding force. Looking back, I am incredibly grateful for the experience of stepping into the unknown. Each obstacle I faced reinforced the importance of perseverance, while each small victory taught me to appreciate the power of taking risks. This journey was not only about professional growth but also about personal transformation. It made me realize the value of embracing life's uncertainties, as these are the very moments that help us grow into the people we are meant to become.

Every day in this new world, I applied the discipline and work ethic instilled in me by the military. But I also learned to adapt, to be adapting and responsive to the ever-changing dynamics of the corporate environment. I came to understand that true success isn't about avoiding risks but about embracing them with open arms. Each challenge, each failure, and each victory became a part of my story, adding depth and character to who I was becoming. I learned to have confidence in myself, to take calculated risks, and to recognize that failures are merely stepping stones on the path to success.

This journey has taught me that the most significant rewards in life often come from the risks we are brave enough to take. It's easy to stay in a comfort zone and choose the path that feels safe and predictable. But growth rarely happens in comfort. It happens when we step into the unknown, willing to face whatever comes our way. By taking this risk, I discovered a renewed sense of purpose and the courage to pursue my dreams. This journey reminded me that life's true meaning lies not in the destination but in the journey itself—in the risks we take, the challenges we face, and the lessons we learn along the way.

In taking this leap, I found a deeper connection with my own strengths and values. I learned that resilience isn't just about endurance; it's about adaptation and growth. It's about having the courage to step into the unknown, even when the path is unclear, and finding a way forward. I also learned that gratitude is a powerful tool in times of uncertainty. It's easy to overlook the small victories and focus only on the end goal. But by practicing gratitude, I learned to appreciate each moment, each lesson, and each experience as a valuable part of my journey.

Today, as I reflect on that leap into civilian life, I am grateful for every challenge and every victory. Each experience has helped shape me into the person I am today, with a renewed sense of purpose and a better vision of what I want to achieve. This journey has taught me that taking risks is not just about pursuing success but about embracing life in all its complexity and beauty. It's about having the courage to step off the beaten path, to trust in oneself, and to forge a path that is uniquely our own.

In the end, this journey was about more than a career change. It was about discovering who I am and what I am capable of. It was about learning to trust myself, to believe in my potential, and to embrace the unknown with a sense of adventure. By taking this leap, I have learned that the most rewarding paths in life are often the ones that are less traveled, the ones that require us to face our fears and take a chance on ourselves. It's a lesson I carry with me every day, a reminder that life's true value lies not in the destination but in the journey itself.

Taking that leap was more than just a decision to leave the military; it was a decision to fully embrace life, with all its uncertainties, challenges, and rewards.

3

THE GOLF LESSON THAT CHANGED MY LIFE

I've always had a firm grip on my goals and a determination to see things through to perfection. For years, I carried the notion that any task worth doing required meticulous planning, full control, and absolute focus on every detail. I learned that mistakes weren't an option from my years in a strict Catholic school and even stricter army training. Success meant reaching the highest standards, no delays, no issues, and no excuses. I believed that this drive would not only benefit my team but create an unbreakable foundation for my own success.

But as time passed, I saw that I was driving myself and my teams to exhaustion. Some things fell beyond my control— unexpected obstacles, people, or circumstances beyond anyone's influence would interfere with what I thought was a perfect plan. And whenever I couldn't reach a goal due to these external limits, I'd internalize it as a personal failure. I quickly blamed myself for the outcome, convinced that my focus, dedication, or work ethic hadn't been enough.

This pressure I put on myself became a constant companion, shaping how I approached every challenge in my life. I fought fiercely against the currents when they pushed back. But one day, a lesson came from an unlikely place: a golf course. I had taken up golf, thinking it would be a relaxing pastime—a game of simple skills that required practice and precision. But golf, as I soon found, was less about control and more about letting go.

Golfing wasn't my first sport. I'd played squash and trained in martial arts regularly, building a fair amount of strength and agility. Golf, like any sport, would be a matter of learning the technique, training the body, and then applying the right amount of strength to make the ball go farther. But nothing could've been further from the truth. My golf lessons began humbly enough as my friends and I lined up with the instructor, listening closely to how to grip the club, align with the target, and swing.

The first time I took the club and lined up for my shot, I thought I'd get it right on my first try. After all, I had the muscle and coordination. But when I swung with all my strength, the ball rolled pathetically just a few feet away. Again, I tried with even more force, determined to show that I could nail this skill if I only put my whole effort into it. But the result was just the same, and my frustration grew.

Watching my friends have some success while I struggled was humbling. I couldn't understand why the harder I tried, the less successful I was. After several attempts, the coach came over and observed my approach. He watched me wind up, adjust, grip tighter, and put everything I had into the swing. He stopped me and said a phrase that would stay with me forever: *"Let go."*

Let go? This was completely counter to my approach, not only in sports but in life. I'd been taught to tighten my grip and hold fast until I reached my goal. But the coach explained that golf was less about power and more about flow. He instructed me to relax my grip, soften my body, and let the swing happen naturally. It felt foreign at first, releasing the tight control I was used to, but when I finally swung with ease, I was shocked. The ball sailed beautifully, finally going where I wanted it to, all because I'd let go.

This simple lesson hit me harder than anything I'd experienced. I thought back to other situations in my life where I'd gripped too hard, forced things, and pushed through to the point of frustration. The lesson was clear: not everything needs a fierce push to succeed. Sometimes, letting go is what opens doors.

EMBRACING FLEXIBILITY OVER FORCE

As I continued practicing golf, I started to see how the idea of "letting go" could echo into other parts of my life, where I often held on to things too tightly. Golf was slowly teaching me to approach situations with a mindset that valued adaptability and flow over brute willpower—a skill that became not just a way to improve my game but a principle to reshape how I lived. I was used to tackling challenges head-on with discipline and rigidity, a habit deeply ingrained by both my strict Catholic upbringing and my time in the military. Every task had to be met with intense focus, strict adherence to the plan, and relentless effort until it was achieved. While this approach had been my formula for strength and success, it had also left me drained and defeated whenever I faced challenges I couldn't overcome by sheer force.

But golf offered a gentler path. Here, there was a concept of letting go, an acceptance of the unknown elements—wind, slope, swing rhythm—that were out of my control. As I became more comfortable with this newfound concept of "letting go," I became more flexible in my approach to life's challenges. I realized flexibility wasn't just about a relaxed grip on the golf club. It was a way of embracing life with resilience and openness, a path to discovering growth and success in areas I had never anticipated.

FLEXIBILITY AS A VIRTUE IN PERSONAL GROWTH

One of the first things I noticed about becoming more flexible was that it allowed me to see things from different perspectives. When I approached golf with a rigid mindset, I thought only of the mechanics—strength, aim, stance. But when I relaxed and followed the flow, the game became an art of adjusting, noticing details in the environment, and responding in a more natural and spontaneous way. This new perspective helped me realize how much I missed when I held too tightly to a goal or a particular way of achieving it. The flexibility allowed me to adapt, assess, and make more authentic and satisfying choices.

In my personal life, this newfound flexibility became a tool for reflection and growth. I started to examine areas where I was too rigid in my expectations of myself and others. In relationships, for example, I had always valued consistency and reliability, seeing these traits as the core of trust and mutual respect. However, in prioritizing these values to an extreme, I often became frustrated with others for not meeting my high standards, and I struggled to forgive myself when I felt I had failed. By embracing flexibility, I realized that growth often requires us to be open to change—not only in others but within ourselves.

When I practiced flexibility, I became more forgiving and understanding. I found it easier to let go of grudges and to accept the imperfections in myself and others. This shift in perspective didn't weaken my principles; instead, it enriched them. It reminded me that true strength comes not from control but from understanding when to hold on and when to let go.

FLEXIBILITY IN CAREER AND DECISION-MAKING

The lessons of flexibility extended beyond personal growth and into my career as well. Before I embraced flexibility, I approached work with a rigid mindset that valued meticulous planning and strict timelines. In my mind, success was defined by efficiency and the ability to foresee and control every possible outcome. But as life often proves, the professional world is filled with unforeseen obstacles, and attempting to control every detail only leads to burnout and frustration.

With a flexible mindset, however, I began to see challenges as opportunities for growth and adaptation. I learned to prioritize the "big picture" over the minute details. Flexibility allowed me to pivot, to adapt quickly, and to let go of plans that no longer served my goals. It helped me build resilience to see each setback not as a failure but as a chance to reassess and improve. This adaptability became one of my greatest strengths, allowing me to stay grounded even when things didn't go according to plan.

One particular experience stands out as a testament to the power of flexibility in decision-making. In my earlier years, I had set a rigid career trajectory for myself, determined to reach a specific position within a certain timeframe. But despite my efforts, I faced setbacks that seemed beyond my control. Instead of pushing harder, I applied what I had learned from golf—stepping back, observing, and adjusting my approach. When I looked at my situation from a new perspective, I realized there were alternate paths I could take to reach my goals. By allowing myself to be flexible, I discovered new opportunities and learned to appreciate the journey itself, not just the destination.

FLEXIBILITY AS A PATH TO RESILIENCE

I've come to realize that resilience is the ability to endure challenges without breaking, and flexibility is its foundation. When we rigidly cling to our expectations, any disruption feels like a personal failure. But when we embrace flexibility, we can absorb life's shocks gracefully and maintain our focus even in the face of adversity. Flexibility transforms resilience from mere endurance into an adaptive strength that helps us navigate uncertainty with confidence.

In golf, resilience is the ability to keep going after a missed shot and to adapt to the next swing without carrying the weight of frustration. In life, this resilience allows us to bounce back from setbacks, not by forcing solutions but by staying open to new approaches. I learned that when things don't go as planned, flexibility enables us to see past immediate disappointments, envision new paths forward, and respond in ways that keep us aligned with our larger goals.

This mindset of flexibility and resilience has been instrumental in helping me navigate change with optimism and patience. In professional settings, it enabled me to respond to changing environments without panic and to stay focused on long-term objectives even when the path forward seemed unclear. In my personal life, flexibility has allowed me to experience a greater sense of peace, knowing that I don't have to control every outcome to find fulfillment.

FLEXIBILITY AND PROBLEM SOLVING

Another powerful benefit of flexibility is how it enhances problem-solving. When we approach challenges with a rigid mindset, we tend to limit ourselves to a narrow set of solutions, often overlooking more influential or innovative options. Flexibility, however, encourages us to think creatively, consider alternate paths, and remain open to new ideas. This creative approach to problem-solving has proven invaluable in both my personal and professional life.

In the military, where precision and discipline are key, there are situations that require quick thinking and adaptability. I've seen firsthand how rigid adherence to protocol can sometimes hinder problem-solving, leading to missed opportunities or inefficient solutions. Embracing flexibility allowed me to break free from the constraints of "the way things are done" and to explore new approaches that led to more effective outcomes.

In golf, too, flexibility is essential. Each hole presents a unique challenge, requiring different strategies and techniques. Sometimes, even the best-laid plans fall short, and a simple adjustment—whether in grip, stance, or mental focus —can make all the difference. Golf taught me to approach problems not with frustration but with curiosity and to view obstacles as opportunities to adapt and grow. This approach has allowed me to see issues from multiple perspectives, leading to solutions I might have overlooked if I had stubbornly clung to a single way of doing things.

FLEXIBILITY AND LETTING GO OF PERFECTIONISM

Perfectionism was a deeply ingrained trait I carried for most of my life. I believed that every task, every project, and every goal required an uncompromising level of precision and flawlessness. But over time, this perfectionism became a heavy burden, leading to stress and disappointment whenever I inevitably fell short of my own high standards.

Golf became a liberating practice in this regard, teaching me that perfection is an illusion and that sometimes, good enough is better than perfect. By allowing myself to make mistakes, to have off days, and to simply enjoy the game, I freed myself from the constant pressure to be flawless. I realized that progress and growth were more fulfilling than perfection and that letting go of perfectionism allowed me to approach each challenge with a healthier, more sustainable mindset.

In life, as in golf, flexibility allows us to embrace imperfection. It helps us to accept that setbacks and mistakes are part of the journey, not indicators of failure. This shift in mindset has allowed me to experience a more profound sense of satisfaction and fulfillment, knowing that I don't have to be perfect to succeed. Flexibility has given me the freedom to pursue my goals with passion and resilience without the need for constant validation or approval.

FLEXIBILITY AS A GUIDE TO LIVING FULLY

Ultimately, flexibility has become a guiding principle in my life, one that has transformed how I approach everything from personal relationships to professional goals. It has shown me that life is not a linear path, but a dynamic journey filled with unexpected twists and turns. By embracing flexibility, I have learned to live more fully, appreciate each moment as it comes, and find joy in growth and discovery.

Flexibility has taught me that there is strength in surrender, in knowing when to release control and let life unfold naturally. It has shown me that the pursuit of success doesn't require unrelenting force but rather a willingness to adapt, learn, and flow with the currents of change. Just as in golf, where each swing is a balance of control and release, life, too, is a dance between effort and surrender, a journey that rewards those who are willing to let go and embrace the beauty of the unknown.

Expanding on this, flexibility becomes not just a virtue but a cornerstone for navigating a meaningful life—one that is resilient, fulfilling, and open to the endless possibilities that lie beyond our immediate vision.

REAL-LIFE SCENARIOS OF "LETTING GO"

One scenario stands out as I reflect on this lesson. Years ago, I worked in a Southeast Asian country, well-positioned within an organization and handling a large team. We'd accomplished complex tasks, overcome seemingly impossible goals, and achieved what many would consider "success." But as the years passed, I felt the call for something more challenging, and I set my sights on a promotion. I'd put my entire energy and drive into this goal, but there was an obstacle: the position was already filled.

Instead of letting go of this goal, I doubled down, contemplating moving to a new company in pursuit of advancement. Eventually, I received an offer for a promising role abroad. However, as fate would have it, a harsh fever hit me the day before my assessment tests. I was in poor shape, but I stubbornly pressed on, traveling sick and exhausted to take the tests. As expected, I failed. This setback stung deeply, and the feeling of failure lingered.

In hindsight, if I'd had the "Chronopath" watch that I'd envisioned in my book—a device that showed me future paths— it would have revealed that my role in my current company would soon evolve on its own. Not long after, the position I'd been vying for opened up naturally, and I was promoted without forcing anything. This experience underscored a powerful truth: sometimes, the right path reveals itself when we stop trying to control every detail.

APPLYING THE LESSON BEYOND THE GOLF COURSE

The more I reflected on that simple yet profound golf lesson, the more I saw its deeper significance. Golf isn't just about technical precision; it's about harmonizing intention with release and effort with freedom. Life, too, is a balance between taking action and surrendering to forces beyond our control. The golf swing became a metaphor, a constant reminder that true success often comes not from relentless control but from a graceful balance between focus and flexibility. It became clear to me that letting go doesn't mean surrendering to passivity or abandoning ambition; it means learning to recognize when to ease up and let things flow as they will.

In personal and professional settings, "letting go" is transformative. It allows us to adapt when circumstances shift, remain open to unexpected opportunities, and discover solutions we might miss when we're too focused on a single outcome. The irony is that by loosening our grip, we often end up achieving our goals with far less frustration and anxiety. The act of letting go, I discovered, doesn't just make life easier—it makes us more capable, resilient, and wise.

Here are some ways that applying this lesson has reshaped my life in powerful and unexpected ways.

LEARNING THE VALUE OF PATIENCE AND TIMING

One of the key takeaways from the golf lesson was that timing, rather than brute strength, is often the key to success. Swinging too hard, too soon, or too forcefully can throw the entire game off. Similarly, in life, pushing too hard, especially when conditions aren't optimal, can lead to disappointment or setbacks. Golf taught me to value patience and timing, two principles that extended into my career and personal endeavors.

For instance, early in my career, I believed that advancement would come from relentless hard work and constant demonstration of my abilities. But after a series of missed opportunities and exhaustion from pushing myself too hard, I realized that sometimes, holding back can be just as important as moving forward. The best timing for new opportunities often comes when we've allowed ourselves to grow, reflect, and prepare rather than simply charging forward without pause. Like in golf, where waiting for the correct alignment creates a smooth, powerful swing, waiting for the right moment in life can lead to success that feels almost effortless.

EMBRACING THE UNKNOWN: THE BENEFITS OF A LOOSER GRIP ON LIFE'S OUTCOMES

Golf, like life, is inherently unpredictable. Wind direction, terrain, and unexpected bounces of the ball add an element of chance to the game. I learned quickly that clinging to exact outcomes—such as expecting every shot to be perfect —only led to frustration. Letting go, releasing expectations, and embracing unpredictability helped me approach each shot with a sense of curiosity rather than dread. This openness to the unknown proved invaluable in other areas of my life as well.

In my career, I used to have a set, inflexible plan for where I wanted to be in five years. But life has a way of throwing curveballs, and opportunities often come from unexpected sources. By loosening my grip on fixed outcomes, I became more open to exploring different paths, which led me to roles and projects I hadn't initially considered but found deeply rewarding. By approaching the future with a sense of curiosity rather than fear, I discovered a more adventurous and fulfilling path than the one I'd meticulously planned.

THE POWER OF ADJUSTING AND ADAPTING

Golf requires constant adjustments—whether it's the club's angle, the swing's force, or the positioning of your feet. This need for adaptation taught me that flexibility is as crucial to success as persistence. Life, too, demands that we stay adaptable, adjusting our plans as circumstances change. Learning to pivot rather than sticking rigidly to an initial plan has helped me navigate career transitions, relationship dynamics, and personal growth with greater ease and effectiveness.

I remember a project at work that initially seemed straightforward. We had clear goals, a tight timeline, and a motivated team. But as we progressed, unexpected challenges arose: changes in market conditions, resource shortages, and shifting client needs. My initial approach was to push forward as planned, but this only created unnecessary stress. Instead, I drew from the golf lesson, reminding myself to adjust, adapt, and go with the flow. We completed the project successfully by recalibrating our goals, involving the team in brainstorming alternative approaches, and focusing on solutions rather than problems, even if the outcome differed from the original vision. This experience underscored the importance of flexibility and openness to change—a lesson I carry with me in all areas of life.

THE PARADOX OF CONTROL: FINDING FREEDOM IN LETTING GO

In both golf and life, I discovered a paradox: the more we try to control every aspect, the less control we seem to have over the outcome. The game taught me that true control comes from the ability to let go when necessary, to relinquish the need for perfect precision and embrace the natural rhythm of the swing. This realization transformed my relationships, my work, and even my mental well-being.

In relationships, for instance, I realized that trying to control every interaction or expecting others to conform to my ideas of how things "should be" only created tension. By letting go of these expectations, I began to foster relationships that were more authentic and enjoyable. In my career, too, I learned that trusting in others and delegating effectively—rather than micromanaging—allowed my team to flourish and led to far better results than if I'd attempted to control every detail myself. The freedom I found in letting go of control has opened my life to experiences, connections, and achievements that would have been out of reach had I clung to a rigid path.

FINDING JOY IN THE PROCESS RATHER THAN THE OUTCOME

When I first began golfing, I focused solely on the end goal—getting the ball in the hole in as few strokes as possible. This single-minded focus led to frustration when things didn't go as planned. Over time, however, I began to appreciate the experience of the game itself. Every swing, every walk across the course, every recalibration became a moment of learning and growth. I discovered that there was joy in the process, not just in the outcome.

This lesson translated beautifully into my daily life. Rather than viewing my personal and professional goals as hurdles to overcome, I started to see them as journeys to savor.

Whether it's the process of working on a long-term project, developing a skill, or nurturing relationships, I learned to appreciate the journey, with all its ups and downs. This shift in focus from the destination to the path made life infinitely more prosperous and more rewarding.

DEVELOPING RESILIENCE THROUGH ACCEPTANCE

Golf taught me another valuable lesson about resilience. In the game, there are days when nothing seems to go right. You miss shots you've practiced countless times, the wind doesn't cooperate, or the course conditions are less than ideal. In life, too, we face moments of adversity that seem to defy our efforts. I learned that resilience isn't about forcing things to go my way but about accepting circumstances and continuing to move forward with a positive mindset.

This perspective has been incredibly helpful in handling life's inevitable challenges. Instead of becoming frustrated by setbacks, I now try to view them as temporary and focus on what I can control—my attitude and my response. This approach has not only strengthened my resilience but also helped me navigate difficult times with a greater sense of calm and clarity.

THE INFLUENCE OF FLEXIBILITY ON CREATIVITY AND PROBLEM-SOLVING

In both golf and life, letting go fosters creativity. When I stopped trying to control every swing, I discovered new techniques and approaches to my game. Similarly, in work and personal projects, letting go of rigid plans opened my mind to creative solutions. Flexibility has been essential in problem-solving, enabling me to consider ideas and perspectives I might have dismissed otherwise.

I remember a work project where a complex problem seemed unsolvable. My initial response was to double down, trying the same approaches more forcefully. But drawing from my golf experience, I took a step back and encouraged the team to brainstorm freely without worrying about immediate solutions. This openness led to a breakthrough that not only solved the issue but inspired innovations we hadn't previously considered. Letting go of rigidity allowed us to tap into a level of creativity that reshaped our approach and improved our outcomes.

CULTIVATING INNER PEACE THROUGH LETTING GO

One of the most unexpected gifts of letting go has been a sense of inner peace. By releasing the need to control every outcome, I've experienced a more profound sense of calm and contentment. In golf, letting go of perfectionism freed me from frustration, enabling me to enjoy the game. In life, the same principle has allowed me to approach each day with a sense of openness and gratitude.

This sense of peace has transformed my approach to challenges. Instead of dreading obstacles or worrying about the future, I've learned to take things as they come, trusting in my ability to adapt and find solutions as needed. By letting go of unnecessary pressure, I've cultivated a mindset that is both proactive and patient, allowing me to navigate life with a grounded sense of purpose.

Ultimately, the lesson I learned on the golf course was about much more than improving my swing. It was a philosophy of life, a reminder that sometimes the best way to achieve our goals is by loosening our grip, letting go, and allowing life to unfold in its own way. I have found a deeper sense of fulfillment, success, and joy than I ever imagined through flexibility, patience, and a willingness to embrace the unknown.

A Thought Experiment

"If this was the last day of your life, would you spend it the way you're spending today?"

— *OPRAH WINFREY*

The Chronopath may be a fictional watch, but it's been a powerful tool of self-discovery for me, and I hope that the process of hearing about my experiences is helping you to reflect on your own life. I mentioned the idea of The Chronopath showing you your final chapter at the very beginning of our journey together, and we'll look at this concept in more depth towards the end of the book... but right now, I'd like to ask you to think about this in a very specific context.

If you knew that tomorrow was your last day on earth, what would you plan to do with it? Let's say you knew that you'd be in good health on that day and you could use it as you wished. You're still scheduled to be at work, but in the light of this knowledge, would you show up? Would you spend time with your family and friends instead? Would you go somewhere that you've always wanted to go? Would you withdraw your savings and use it to fund your final day?

You will never know for sure when your last day will be, but asking yourself these questions will tell you a lot about your priorities. What truly matters to you? The answers may not allow you to change your life—after all, you still have to earn money and do particular things to survive and be well—but they may give you a better idea of the things you'd really like your life to be about. This thought exercise alone can give you a lot of direction.

I wanted to draw your attention to this at this moment specifically because I wanted to bring your focus back to your own life for a second. I hope that my story will bring you ways to reflect on your own life, but I also want to challenge you to do this explicitly. It's been such a powerful journey for me, and I'd love to be able to help you too.

This is really the main reason this book came into existence. Although it's a memoir, the driving force behind it was to share what my explorations of The Chronopath have taught me in the hopes that they might help other people. So, while you're taking this moment to reflect, I'd also like to invite you to help me share it with a wider audience.

By leaving a review of this book on Amazon, you'll make it easier for new readers to find it and find their own pathways to a life that truly fulfills them.

We all read reviews when we're looking for new reading material, and a few words from you could make a real difference in connecting this book with the people it will resonate with the most.

Thank you so much for your support. I truly appreciate it. Please keep mulling over this idea of what you'd do with one last day—it will help you when we get to Chapter 5 and start thinking about the fleeting nature of time.

$$4$$

CROSSROADS IN MY LIFE

As the days drift into weeks and weeks into years, we often fail to notice time's quiet but constant passage. Daily routines create a sense of continuity, a security that tomorrow will look much like today, with the same tasks and goals waiting for us. In my case, this rhythm had become so ingrained that years had flown by without me truly realizing it. By the time I paused to look back, I found myself well into my fifties, living under the same pressures and demands as I had decades before, still shouldering the weight of deadlines, yearly targets, and high-stakes projects.

It was as though I had spent a lifetime sprinting in a marathon with no end. Each passing year in the corporate world came with its achievements, but also with the ever-present demands for growth and increased productivity. Every accomplishment was celebrated with barely a pause, because in no time, the next target loomed large. And with each goal achieved, there was another, as if the finish line kept moving farther away. The work was rewarding: I felt a sense of pride and purpose in guiding teams to achieve challenging objectives, problem-solving, and building something greater than myself. But as time passed, that same work began to feel like a relentless current, dragging me along without asking if this was the journey I wanted.

At its core, corporate life is a machine—a system designed to generate success, profit, and innovation. Individuals like me play our roles, contributing time, energy, and health to keep that machine moving. For years, I did just that, thriving within the structure, driven by the sense that my contributions were valuable and my presence indispensable. The machine didn't care about personal milestones, time with family, or even personal well-being; it simply moved forward, demanding more from those within its gears. There were promotions and raises, accolades and meetings, but I had given so much of myself that I began to feel more like a cog in that machine than a person with a life outside it.

I realized that time is a currency we can never get back. With each hour and each day, I was spending mine, and someday, that currency would run out entirely. I could not reclaim it, nor could I choose to save it for a later date. This was not something that could be bought back, no matter how much I earned or how many promotions I achieved. Each day, I found myself asking, *How much longer can I keep giving without really living?*

The corporate machine is a vast, unfeeling structure that does not pause for individuals, regardless of their dedication or sacrifice. Companies are built on the foundation of growth—quarterly profits, year-over-year success, and revenue that must always increase. While that structure serves the organization's purpose, for those within it, there is an inevitable cost: time, energy, and an increasing sense of distance from personal happiness and freedom. The corporation grows, but the individual within can feel as if they are shrinking as if their own life is being sacrificed at the altar of progress.

In my decades of work, I have achieved many of the goals I had set out to reach. From junior roles to leadership, I moved up the ladder with determination and focus. I poured my energy into every project, every team I led, and every objective I was assigned. There were many moments of fulfillment—guiding a team through tough challenges, seeing them succeed, or bringing a project to fruition. The problem was that every step I took seemed to come with a greater demand on my time, my focus, and my personal life. The higher I climbed, the more I became a part of the corporate machine, an essential part, yes, but one that could be replaced if it didn't perform as expected.

As much as I enjoyed the work, I began to feel a gnawing sense of emptiness, realizing that while giving all I had to my career, my own life was passing me by. My time was being spent, and one day, there would be none left. *What did I have to show for it?* A decorated résumé and financial stability, yes —but what about personal fulfillment? What about those small, everyday moments that bring joy and contentment? I often put off those things, thinking that one day I would have time for them once I reached the next milestone or promotion.

The truth is, the time to enjoy life doesn't magically appear when you reach a certain point in your career. It has to be intentionally carved out, protected, and valued. Otherwise, it is all too easy to become consumed by work demands, swept along by the current until there is no time left to course-correct. Corporate life offers many rewards, but it rarely provides the time to truly reflect, recalibrate, or pursue happiness on our own terms.

For years, I had ignored the subtle signs—the fatigue that took longer to shake, the anxiety that crept in even during moments of rest, and the feeling that I was on a treadmill that would never stop. But as I reached my mid-fifties, the signs became impossible to ignore. I began to notice that, each month, I was hearing about the passing of former colleagues, friends, and even mentors. These were people I had once worked alongside and laughed with, people who had been just as dedicated, just as committed to their work as I was. Their deaths came as reminders that time is not something we can afford to waste. It is finite, unpredictable, and precious beyond measure.

These losses made me wonder: *What if I am next? What have I truly done with my time?* It wasn't fear, exactly, but an urgent need to reevaluate my life's direction to determine if I was living in a way that honored the time I had left. I had responsibilities, of course—my family, my loved ones, the people who depended on me. There were obligations I had taken on to ensure their security and well-being. But I couldn't shake the sense that I had given so much of myself to these obligations that I had lost sight of my own happiness and fulfillment.

Much of my life had been spent pursuing goals for the future. I worked tirelessly to provide for my family, give my children the best possible education, and ensure a stable life for those I cared about. I thought of my dream to travel, see the world, and enjoy the fruits of my labor once I retired. But as time passed, that future seemed to recede, always just beyond reach, as if the very act of working for tomorrow made it impossible to truly live today.

The corporate world creates a sense of urgency, a culture of perpetual "next steps." There is always something to achieve, a target to meet, and a milestone to celebrate before moving on to the next. We tell ourselves that we will pause *once we get there*, that we will enjoy life once we reach a certain point, only to find that there is always another goal waiting just beyond it. It is an endless loop, one that can easily consume our best years if we let it.

The turning point came when I found myself deeply exhausted, both physically and mentally. I began to feel that I had given all I could offer, that I was pouring from an empty cup. Achievements were no longer enough to sustain me; the satisfaction of a job well done had lost its appeal. I realized that I needed to step back and take a break, not just for my health but for my soul. It was time to pause, to recalibrate, and to chart a new course—one that was not defined by corporate milestones or the demands of a never-ending workload.

At that moment, I began to see my life as a series of crossroads. Each decision, each moment of choice, had led me to this point. And now, I was at another crossroads, one where I had the power to choose a different path, one that honored the time I had left. I no longer wanted to spend my days in service of someone else's goals; I wanted to live on my own terms, find a way of being that allowed me to savor each moment, and appreciate the simple pleasures that I had so often overlooked.

Looking at my imaginary Chronopath—a symbolic tool I had conceived to remind myself of life's fleeting nature—I saw that the future was uncertain and that the time to make meaningful changes was now. I wanted to do work that mattered, yes, but also work that allowed me to live fully, to be present with my family, to pursue passions that had long been neglected. It was a daunting decision, one that required courage and faith, but it was also one of the most liberating choices I had ever made.

Quitting my job felt like stepping off a speeding train, allowing myself to catch my breath and look around. I was no longer bound by the demands of the corporate machine; I was free to choose how I spent my days, to prioritize my own happiness and well-being. The obligations were still there, of course—family, responsibilities, the things that truly mattered—but now I had the freedom to approach them on my own terms.

This new era in my life was not about abandoning purpose but redefining it. I wanted to find work that aligned with my values, and that allowed me to make a difference without sacrificing my time and well-being. I wanted to slow down, savor each day, and be present in ways I had never been able to before. I wanted to take control of my life, to live intentionally rather than letting the demands of the day dictate my path.

The journey of redefinition was not easy, and it took time to happen. But each day, I found myself growing closer to a sense of fulfillment that I had not felt in years. I had spent so long serving external goals that I had lost sight of what truly mattered. Now, with the gift of time and freedom, I could begin to rediscover those things to rebuild a life that honored my own values and aspirations.

The crossroads in my life led me to this new path, one defined not by corporate milestones but by personal meaning and fulfillment. It was a journey of self-discovery, learning to let go of the demands that had once controlled me, and embracing a life that was truly my own.

REDISCOVERING VALUES AND PERSONAL ALIGNMENT

For so many years, I had allowed my values to be shaped by the company I worked for, the projects I managed, and the targets I met. I had always thought that aligning with corporate goals was just part of the job, a small sacrifice for what seemed like significant achievements. But at this new crossroads, I realized that my values had become blurred and distant, obscured by years of prioritizing productivity over peace and results over reflection.

The journey to rediscover my values was neither immediate nor easy. It began with quiet reflection—time spent revisiting the core beliefs that had once inspired me before they were eclipsed by deadlines and KPIs. I have always valued creativity, freedom, and the opportunity to make a meaningful impact on the people around me. But in my former life, these values had been sidelined by the pressures of bottom lines and quarterly results.

As I sifted through my values, one truth became clear: I wanted to work in ways that allowed me to be present. The corporate hustle had often demanded my presence in meetings and projects yet left me feeling strangely absent from my own life. Now, I sought work that offered the freedom to slow down, engage fully with my surroundings, and experience life without feeling tethered to someone else's agenda.

REDEFINING SUCCESS AND ACHIEVEMENT

One of the most challenging aspects of my transition was reimagining what success meant to me. For over three decades, success has been defined by promotions, achievements, and the upward climb through an organization. Each goal met was followed by a new one, a continual chain that seemed endless. But as I stood at this crossroads, I realized that my definition of success needed an overhaul.

In this new phase of life, success was no longer about titles or accolades. It became about inner contentment, about waking up each morning without the familiar dread of rushing toward a new deadline. I began to measure success not by the hours I worked or the projects I completed but by the joy I felt, the peace I cultivated, and the personal goals I accomplished outside of a professional setting.

This redefinition of success was both liberating and humbling. It meant accepting that the corporate world's version of achievement was no longer my compass. Instead, I focused on personal growth, building relationships, and pursuing passions that had nothing to do with productivity or profit. The idea of success evolved from being "the best" at something to simply "being" in each moment fully and appreciatively.

THE ART OF INTENTIONAL LIVING

Intentional living became my new mantra. After years of letting corporate schedules shape my life, I was eager to live with purpose on my own terms. But intentionality required discipline and a conscious departure from ingrained habits. I had to unlearn the reflex of filling every moment with tasks and the mindset that idle time was wasted time.

Intentional living meant saying "no" more often than I was accustomed to. I learned to prioritize the things that truly mattered:

- Spending quality time with my family
- Cultivating friendships
- Nurturing hobbies I'd long neglected

I also set aside time for reflection, allowing myself to simply sit with my thoughts—a practice once foreign to me, as back-to-back tasks governed my days.

By living intentionally, I found a sense of control that had eluded me in my career-driven life. I no longer felt pulled in a thousand directions; instead, I felt grounded, clear in my priorities, and free to spend my time in ways that genuinely resonated with my values. In doing so, I rediscovered a level of peace and fulfillment that I had thought was lost to me.

LEARNING TO SAVOR LIFE'S SIMPLE PLEASURES

One of the greatest joys of this new path was rediscovering life's simple pleasures—those small moments that we often overlook in the rush of daily life. In my corporate years, I scarcely took a moment to truly savor anything. Meals were eaten quickly, sunsets were mere background, and weekends were spent recuperating rather than experiencing life.

As I embraced this new era, I deliberately tried to slow down and notice the details I had once ignored. I learned to savor my morning coffee, not just as a quick boost but as a moment of quiet solitude. I found joy in taking long walks, marveling at the changing seasons, and watching the natural world unfold in its own rhythm. These simple pleasures became my reminders to live mindfully, remain present, and appreciate the beauty in ordinary moments.

Learning to savor life, I found a profound gratitude for the world around me. No longer was I consumed by future goals or deadlines; I could be fully present in each moment, appreciating life in a new and deeply fulfilling way.

EMBRACING THE POWER OF REFLECTION AND GROWTH

This era of my life was marked by constant reflection, a process I had once overlooked in the race to keep up with professional demands. But now, reflection has become my compass, guiding me to a deeper understanding of myself and my place in the world. I reflected on past decisions, on lessons learned, and on the ways I wanted to grow moving forward.

Reflection also offered me a chance to reassess my beliefs, my attitudes, and my goals. I no longer saw growth as synonymous with career advancement; instead, it was about personal development, emotional resilience, and spiritual well-being. This kind of growth was not measured in promotions or titles but in how connected I felt to my values and how much I learned from life's experiences.

Through reflection, I discovered a newfound commitment to personal growth that went beyond professional goals. It was about becoming a more compassionate, thoughtful, and present person. It was about cultivating qualities that made life more prosperous and more meaningful, far beyond any corporate achievement.

FINDING BALANCE BETWEEN GIVING AND RECEIVING

The corporate world had instilled in me a habit of constant giving—giving time, energy, and focus to meet demands and achieve results. But in this new phase of life, I learned that balance required both giving and receiving. I needed to give to others in meaningful ways, but I also needed to give to myself the time and attention I had so often neglected.

Finding balance was not just about saying no to professional demands; it was also about learning to receive joy, welcome rest, and embrace moments of quiet. It was a shift from always pushing forward to learning to be content with stillness. This balance allowed me to recharge, approach each day with fresh energy and enthusiasm, and feel whole in a way that had been elusive for so many years.

DISCOVERING THE JOY OF PERSONAL FULFILLMENT

As I journeyed down this new path, I found that fulfillment came not from external validation but from within. Personal fulfillment became my goal—finding joy in creative pursuits, engaging in hobbies that brought me peace, and spending time with loved ones without the looming pressure of corporate tasks.

I realized that true fulfillment came from living a life that reflected my values and passions, not from the accolades or recognition that had once motivated me. This sense of satisfaction was quiet and profound, unbound by external expectations or demands. It was a joy that stemmed from simply being present, from knowing that I was living authentically, true to myself.

EMBRACING THE UNKNOWN WITH OPEN ARMS

At this new crossroads, I had to face the unknown—a future that was no longer mapped out by a company or defined by set goals. This uncertainty was both daunting and exhilarating. I didn't know exactly where this path would lead, but for the first time, I was okay with that. I learned to embrace the unknown with a sense of curiosity and to view each day as an opportunity to discover something new about myself and the world around me.

Letting go of the need for a clear plan was liberating. I was free to explore new interests, to take risks without fearing the repercussions on my career, and to redefine what success looked like with each passing day. The unknown became a canvas, a space where I could create my own story, unfettered by the demands of a corporate life.

BUILDING A LEGACY BEYOND PROFESSIONAL SUCCESS

As I walked along this new path, the question of legacy became increasingly present. It felt like a natural part of stepping back from the corporate demands that had shaped so much of my life. But this time, my idea of legacy shifted; it was no longer tethered to the milestones of my career or the accolades I had amassed. Instead, it became a deeply personal pursuit, rooted in what I would leave behind as a person—not as a corporate figure or a résumé full of accomplishments, but as someone who truly lived with purpose and joy.

Reflecting on my legacy, I realized I wanted it to be something meaningful beyond titles, beyond job descriptions, and beyond any external validation. I wanted to leave a legacy of love, kindness, and joy—one that people close to me would carry forward as part of their own lives. This new vision wasn't about being remembered for managing successful projects or hitting ambitious goals but rather about being remembered as someone who enriched the lives of others. It was about creating lasting memories with family and friends, fostering meaningful connections, and genuinely contributing to the well-being of the people around me.

THE SHIFT FROM PROFESSIONAL SUCCESS TO PERSONAL HAPPINESS

For so long, my focus has been on achieving professional success. I'd built my life around the pursuit of excellence, climbing ladders, and gathering the accolades that marked me as a high achiever. In many ways, I believed that each milestone achieved, each promotion accepted, would contribute to an enduring sense of fulfillment. Yet, with every new accomplishment, I found the satisfaction to be fleeting—a temporary rush of pride or validation that quickly dissolved with the onset of a new deadline or the next ambitious target. It was a pattern that repeated over and over, each time leaving me wanting more but never feeling fully content. The truth was becoming clear: professional success and true happiness weren't one and the same.

In the fast-paced, goal-oriented environment of corporate life, happiness often seemed like a secondary concern, something that could be addressed "later" after all other demands had been met. But as the years went by, "later" felt increasingly elusive. I started to recognize that if I continued to wait for happiness to emerge from my work, I might end up looking back with regret. This realization spurred a shift in my perspective; I began to understand that genuine happiness doesn't spring from titles, accolades, or the thrill of a completed task. True happiness, I came to see, is rooted in living a life aligned with personal values—a life that brings joy not only to oneself but also to those around us.

A REDEFINITION OF SUCCESS

With this newfound clarity, I began to redefine success on my own terms. Success was no longer about meeting external expectations or proving my worth through professional achievements. Instead, I started to see it as a state of fulfillment derived from authenticity and a life that resonated with my true self. I realized that living authentically meant listening to my inner values rather than being swayed by the pressures of career aspirations or societal norms. This authenticity brought a sense of peace that I hadn't experienced before and, with it, a renewed sense of purpose.

This redefinition of success led me to prioritize aspects of life that I had once overlooked. Building strong relationships, creating memories with loved ones, and making positive contributions to the lives of others began to stand out as the true markers of success. I saw that these were the achievements that would form the foundation of a legacy worth leaving. This shift brought with it a more profound sense of satisfaction than any professional milestone ever had. I no longer felt compelled to climb yet another ladder or push myself to meet the following objective; instead, I found joy in simply living each day with intention.

LETTING GO OF EXTERNAL VALIDATION

One of the most challenging parts of this transition was learning to let go of the need for external validation. In the corporate world, feedback and recognition can become almost addictive; they fuel a sense of accomplishment that's hard to find elsewhere. However, this feedback often comes with conditions—it's granted when a certain goal is met or a task is completed. Realizing that my happiness had become tied to these forms of validation was eye-opening. I understood that as long as I relied on external approval, my sense of fulfillment would be temporary and always contingent on others.

Letting go of this need required self-reflection and a commitment to valuing my own judgment above external praise. I began to focus on what truly made me happy, regardless of whether it was recognized by others or even aligned with what society considered "successful." This change was challenging; it involved rewiring years of habits and learning to trust my instincts. But with time, I discovered that internal validation, derived from living in line with my values, was more enduring and satisfying. By valuing my own opinion over external feedback, I became free to pursue happiness in its purest form—on my own terms.

DISCOVERING HAPPINESS IN RELATIONSHIPS AND CONNECTIONS

One of the most surprising revelations of this journey was the importance of relationships. In the busyness of my career, I had often sacrificed personal connections for the sake of work. While I maintained friendships and family ties, they often took a backseat to deadlines and objectives. As I stepped away from this work-centered mindset, I found myself drawn to spending more time with loved ones. I saw that the moments of shared laughter, support, and companionship were more fulfilling than any business achievement could be.

Building and nurturing relationships brought a richness to my life that was both humbling and uplifting. I began to realize that true happiness often lies in the connections we create, the love we share, and the memories we build with those around us. These relationships became my anchor, a source of stability and joy that I could turn to regardless of any professional setback. They reminded me that while accomplishments might bring temporary satisfaction, relationships are what give life meaning. The value of these connections, I understood, would endure far beyond any career or role.

THE ROLE OF GIVING AND CONTRIBUTION

With my focus shifted away from personal achievement, I found a new source of happiness in giving and contributing to others. The fast pace of corporate life had left little room for this aspect of life; most days, my time and energy were devoted to meeting targets rather than helping those in need. But as I began to step back, I saw opportunities to support others in ways that felt meaningful. Whether through mentoring, volunteering, or simply lending a listening ear, I realized that helping others brought me joy that was both profound and lasting.

The act of giving connects us to a purpose greater than ourselves. In contributing to the well-being of others, we cultivate empathy, kindness, and gratitude—qualities that enrich our own lives as much as those we help. This form of happiness was far more sustainable than the fleeting rewards of professional success. It wasn't about being recognized or praised; it was about knowing that my actions, however small, made a positive impact on someone else. This realization strengthened my resolve to live a life focused on kindness and generosity.

EMBRACING SIMPLICITY AND CONTENTMENT

As I embraced this new perspective, I also learned the value of simplicity. In the past, my happiness had been linked to achievement and progress. The idea of "enough" had felt foreign, as if there was always one more goal to reach, one more milestone to accomplish. But with this shift, I began to see that happiness didn't require constant achievement; instead, it could be found in the simple pleasures of daily life. I found joy in quiet moments, in enjoying a sunset, in reading a good book, or in sharing a meal with family.

This simplicity brought a sense of contentment that I had never experienced in my professional pursuits. Contentment is the quiet happiness that arises from appreciating what we already have. It's a state of being at peace with oneself and the world rather than constantly striving for more. Embracing simplicity allowed me to focus on the present moment rather than being consumed by future goals. It taught me that happiness doesn't always require extraordinary achievements; sometimes, it's simply about being fully present in the ordinary moments.

CULTIVATING A LIFE OF PURPOSE AND FULFILLMENT

Ultimately, this shift from professional success to personal happiness led me to a life of purpose and fulfillment. No longer driven by the need to achieve, I found myself motivated by a desire to live authentically and contribute to the well-being of those around me. This journey was a process of rediscovering what truly mattered—values like love, kindness, and integrity—and building a life that reflected them.

Living with purpose meant that my actions were aligned with my beliefs and that I was true to myself in both big decisions and small daily choices. This alignment brought a sense of peace and happiness that felt more genuine than any career accomplishment. In living with purpose, I discovered that happiness isn't a goal to be achieved but a way of life to be embraced. As I continue on this path, I find joy not in external success but in the quiet satisfaction of knowing that I am living in a way that is true to myself and meaningful to others.

In making this shift, I created a life that values people over productivity, relationships over results, and love over accolades. It's a life where happiness is no longer a fleeting feeling tied to external achievements but a steady, enduring presence grounded in the things that truly matter. This shift has been a journey of self-discovery, and while it hasn't been without its challenges, it has led me to a happiness that feels both profound and lasting.

HAPPINESS AS THE FOUNDATION OF A MEANINGFUL LEGACY

When I thought about the people who had left the greatest impact on me, it wasn't their job titles or professional accolades that stood out. Rather, it was the warmth they brought into a room, the way they made others feel valued, and the laughter they shared. These individuals had something in common—they embodied happiness in their daily lives and shared it freely with others. Their happiness wasn't the fleeting kind but a deep, steady joy that came from living in alignment with their purpose and values. They left behind memories of kindness, generosity, and genuine care—qualities that inspired everyone around them.

I realized that happiness, when shared, becomes a powerful force in building a legacy. Happiness uplifts others, fosters connections, and has a ripple effect that can extend far beyond a single person's life. When we live with joy as our guide, we begin to prioritize what truly matters. We make time for loved ones, support others in need, and bring light to moments that would otherwise be ordinary. These are the moments that form the memories people carry with them, and in turn, these memories form the essence of our legacy.

THE JOY OF CREATING LASTING MEMORIES

In pursuing a life focused on happiness, I found myself drawn to creating memories with the people who mattered most. Unlike work accomplishments, memories are enduring; they don't fade with the passing of time but rather grow richer as they're shared and relived. I realized that the happiest moments in my life often had little to do with my professional achievements. Instead, they were times spent laughing with family, sharing stories with friends, and simply enjoying the company of others.

Creating memories became a priority. I made time for family gatherings, prioritized vacations with loved ones, and engaged in conversations that strengthened our connections. I wanted these moments to be my legacy, knowing that they would live on in the minds and hearts of those I cared about. Unlike professional achievements, these memories were tangible expressions of love, joy, and kindness. They were a testament to a life that valued people over productivity and relationships over results.

THE LEGACY OF KINDNESS AND GENEROSITY

In redefining my legacy, kindness and generosity took center stage. Corporate success often emphasizes competition, deadlines, and results, but kindness and generosity focus on giving without expecting anything in return. I wanted my legacy to be one that showed my commitment to these qualities—not just in grand gestures but in the small, consistent ways I could show up for others.

I started to think about how simple acts of kindness can create an enduring impact. A word of encouragement, a genuine compliment, or a listening ear can often mean more to someone than we realize. I made an effort to be there for others, to be a friend, a mentor, or just a person who could offer support. This approach also became a source of happiness for me; in giving to others, I found a deep sense of fulfillment. The joy of kindness became a guiding force, showing me that legacies are not built solely on significant accomplishments but on the small, loving acts we do daily.

CONTRIBUTION TO COMMUNITY: A LASTING IMPACT

Beyond personal connections, I also wanted my legacy to reflect a contribution to the community. I sought ways to give back, to support causes that mattered, and to invest in the well-being of the world beyond my immediate circle.

Contributing to the community became a way to expand my sense of purpose, knowing that I could play a role in making the world a better place, even in small ways. Volunteering, supporting local initiatives, and using my resources to help those in need became part of my new purpose. It was a way of paying forward the opportunities I'd been given and acknowledging that our lives are intertwined.

Contributing to the community added another dimension to my legacy, showing that happiness is not only about personal satisfaction but also about creating a world where others can thrive. I wanted my legacy to reflect the idea that true success is communal and that we are most successful when we lift others up. By focusing on the needs of others, I found that my own sense of happiness and fulfillment grew. Giving back became a source of joy, reminding me that the greatest legacies are those that extend beyond ourselves.

REMEMBERING WHAT TRULY MATTERS

As I moved forward on this path, I became increasingly conscious of the importance of living each day in alignment with what truly mattered. No longer was I focused on meeting others' expectations or striving for achievements that brought temporary satisfaction. Instead, I embraced a life guided by happiness, love, and a commitment to the values I held dear. In doing so, I found a sense of peace and contentment that I hadn't experienced in years.

I realized that a well-lived life is spent in the pursuit of happiness—not just personal happiness, but the happiness we create in others. This happiness is our true legacy; it's what people remember when we're gone, what lives on in their hearts, and what inspires them to live their lives more fully. Happiness is not just a fleeting emotion but a way of being that, when practiced, radiates outward and leaves an enduring impact.

CONCLUSION: CRAFTING A LEGACY OF JOY AND MEANING

Building a legacy beyond professional success means redefining what we leave behind. In my journey, I found that the most meaningful legacy is outside the titles we earn or the projects we complete. It's in the love we share, the kindness we show, and the happiness we bring to others. By focusing on these qualities, I discovered that true fulfillment lies in creating a life that reflects joy, compassion, and a commitment to making the world a little brighter for those around us.

As I continue to walk this path, I do so with the knowledge that every act of love, every moment of kindness, and every instance of shared joy contributes to the legacy I will leave. It's a legacy rooted in the happiness I bring to others, a reminder that our most outstanding achievements are often the simplest, most genuine connections we make. With this understanding, I feel a renewed sense of purpose—one that isn't tied to professional accolades but to the deeper, lasting impact of a life lived with love, joy, and integrity.

A NEW PATH FORWARD

In the end, the crossroads in my life led me to a path defined not by corporate achievements but by personal meaning and fulfillment. It was a journey of self-discovery, learning to let go of the demands that had once controlled me, and embracing a life that was truly my own.

This new journey is ongoing, marked by the daily choice to live intentionally, to be present, and to honor the values that had long been overshadowed. It is a path that demands courage, self-reflection, and the willingness to redefine success in deeply personal terms. With each step, I am reminded that the true measure of a life well-lived lies not in what we achieve but in how we experience each moment, how we touch the lives of others, and how faithfully we live in alignment with our own unique purpose.

The crossroads led me to a new path forward, where each day is a testament to the life I have chosen—a life of balance, fulfillment, and personal freedom.

5

THE LAST CHAPTER IN LIFE

THE FLEETING NATURE OF TIME

As I reflect on my life journey, I am struck by the relentless passage of time. The moments I once thought would last forever now feel like distant echoes, slipping through my fingers as days turned to years. Each milestone—a new job, a relationship, or an accomplishment—felt monumental at the time, but now it all blurs together, giving the impression of an unstoppable flow, as if time is some vast river carrying us forward without a chance to pause and reflect. I think back to my ambitions as a younger person, those bold dreams and aspirations that seemed to reach out endlessly into the future. Yet, somewhere along the way, I stopped keeping track of those dreams, too busy with the tasks and duties of daily life to truly consider where I was going. Now, looking back, I'm filled with wonder at how effortlessly time has slipped by, almost unnoticed, and how little I anticipated its swift movement.

The Chronopath—the imaginary watch that reveals how much time remains—emerged as a powerful symbol of this awareness. A timepiece that doesn't just tick away the seconds, minutes, and hours we have used but instead emphasizes what's left. It urges us to make decisions and to look forward with the same energy we once had as we looked to the past. It forces us to think not just about "one day" in the future but about what truly matters right now. And in a way, it presents a fascinating challenge: if you knew the hours you had remaining, what would you prioritize? What dreams or unfinished goals would resurface? What relationships would you nurture? The Chronopath prompts us to live more intentionally, to find value in each hour and each choice.

THE IMPACT OF TIME AWARENESS

My perspective would shift dramatically if I knew exactly how much time I had left. Let's say the Chronopath tells me I have just one year left. My actions and choices in that year would likely focus on creating memories, spending time with loved ones, and checking off those meaningful items on my personal "bucket list." Each day would feel weighted with significance, a valuable opportunity to live fully. Conversely, if the Chronopath revealed I had five or ten years left, I might feel less urgency, but I would still be conscious of the time remaining, of how precious each day is, and how I might use it wisely. And with twenty years or more, I'd have the room to think even more significant, planning, building, and continuing to pursue goals with more gradual and steady progress.

But this awareness would not just affect how I use my time; it would transform my perception of it. Why? Because knowing the amount of time left forces us to confront our mortality and the limits of our existence. For many, this knowledge could be terrifying; it threatens to bring all our hidden fears and insecurities to the surface. Yet, there's also something liberating in it. To see the boundaries of our lives is to gain a better understanding of what truly matters. It can push us to cut out trivial concerns, prioritize relationships and pursuits that genuinely add value, and live with the sort of intentionality that often escapes us in the day-to-day hustle.

THE PSYCHOLOGY OF TIME AND FULFILLMENT

Our perception of time and the way we value it is deeply psychological. Reflecting on why knowing our "remaining time" would change our behavior brings up some complex feelings. Often, the fear of missed opportunities and regrets looms large when we think about the end of our lives. There's an almost instinctive urge to maximize every moment, to make sure that when we reach the end, we feel no lingering dissatisfaction. But I realize something pivotal here: if we're genuinely content, if we're happy with the path we're on, the number of remaining years doesn't really matter. We would continue living with the same zest and passion, knowing that our choices align with our values and bring us fulfillment.

Many people live their lives as if they're on a path that's been chosen for them, stuck in routines and obligations that they neither enjoy nor find purpose in. This often leads to a situation where they're postponing their real dreams and passions to an imaginary future—someday when they have "enough" time, money, or freedom to pursue what they really love. The Chronopath challenges this postponement mindset, exposing the fallacy of saving life's best for later. If our happiness and satisfaction are dependent on future events that may never come to pass, we're wasting precious time, trapped in an endless cycle of waiting.

This has led me to understand a powerful truth: the time remaining should only matter if we're not fulfilled with our current lives. Otherwise, each day is a chance to do what we love, to be with people who matter, and to cultivate a sense of purpose. Living in this way, where each day holds meaning, would render the countdown of the Chronopath irrelevant. No matter how much or little time I have left, I would face each day with the confidence that I'm living in alignment with my values and purpose.

THE CHALLENGE OF LIVING FULLY IN THE MOMENT

Yet, as simple as it sounds, living this way is challenging. It requires a level of self-awareness, courage, and commitment that many people, myself included, often struggle to maintain. Life has a way of pulling us into distractions, tempting us with superficial achievements and the illusion of endless time. It takes discipline to pull ourselves back to the present, to look beyond the immediate pressures, and to remember the bigger picture. The Chronopath could serve as a constant reminder of the importance of living now. It would whisper to us in moments of doubt or distraction, reminding us that time is finite and urging us to reconnect with our values and purpose.

The beauty of this imaginary watch is that it doesn't change time itself; it changes our relationship with it. Instead of fearing time's passage, we would embrace it, using each tick of the clock as a guide toward living authentically. With the Chronopath, the focus shifts from "I'll do it someday" to "I'll do it today because time waits for no one." It's a gentle yet profound push toward living mindfully, savoring each experience, and letting go of unnecessary worries.

A LIFE OF CONTINUOUS PRESENCE AND PURPOSE

If I were to live my life as though I had my Chronopath at my side, I would work to carry this perspective into every aspect of my day. It's a way of life that recognizes the present as the only guaranteed moment we have. With this watch, I could let go of regrets about the past and anxiety about the future, grounding myself in the now. Imagine the peace that would come from focusing only on what's in front of you, unburdened by the uncertainties of tomorrow. Each interaction and task would take on new significance as an irreplaceable piece of a much larger journey.

When we live with this mindset, we cultivate what could be described as a "chronopath mentality"—a way of being that values every moment and seeks purpose in the present. This mindset doesn't depend on knowing exactly when the end will come but rather on the conscious choice to live fully within each day's boundaries. It's about finding joy and fulfillment in the little things, treating each moment as though it were the culmination of all that came before and a prelude to all that is yet to come.

EMBRACING THE IMPERMANENCE OF TIME

Ultimately, time's fleeting nature is a gift. Its impermanence gives life its shape, providing a framework within which we make choices, experience love, endure hardship, and find meaning. Without an end date, life would lose its urgency and poignancy. The knowledge that time is finite, whether given to us by a Chronopath or our own reflections, creates a sense of importance that drives us to live deeply and purposefully.

In embracing this concept, I find comfort. The time we have may be fleeting, but it's precisely this transience that allows us to see what's most valuable. The days, years, and decades may slip by, but if we live with awareness, gratitude, and purpose, we can look back on our journey with a sense of pride and satisfaction, knowing that we truly lived in each moment.

In this way, the Chronopath is more than just an imaginary device; it's a philosophy, a reminder that time is constantly slipping by. It urges us to decide what's next, to savor each day, and to live fully, making every tick of the clock a part of the story we'll leave behind.

THE ILLUSION OF "SOMEDAY"

The idea of postponing happiness and fulfillment until a future "someday" is woven deeply into the fabric of our culture. We hear it in expressions like "I'll be happy when…"

or "One day, I'll finally…". It's as if satisfaction is a destination we'll reach once we've ticked enough boxes or accomplished a series of lofty goals. This mindset is subtly reinforced in the stories we're told and the goals we set for ourselves, creating a collective notion that life's natural treasures are always waiting just over the horizon. But as I've reflected on my own life, I've come to see this mindset as a kind of mental trap, a clever mechanism we use to defer our enjoyment of life, forever pushing true living into the future.

This "someday" thinking becomes a mechanism to justify our choices, telling ourselves that enduring today's challenges will be worth it for tomorrow's rewards. We constantly gather, build, and acquire things, hoping that one day, we'll sit back and appreciate everything we've accumulated. But this approach often results in a life spent amassing without genuinely enjoying. We push through struggles, convincing ourselves that the hardships are temporary, part of a grander plan that will bring satisfaction in the end. Yet, looking back, I realize how often this pursuit of "someday" has felt like an unending race, a journey based on an imaginary timeline with arbitrary "X" and "Y" dates for beginning and end.

THE ENDLESS CYCLE OF POSTPONEMENT

The pursuit of "someday" creates a cycle that, once started, can be difficult to break. We convince ourselves that reaching certain goals will finally allow us to relax, yet upon reaching them, we quickly replace them with new ones. This endless cycle of postponement can make life feel like a marathon with no finish line, where satisfaction is persistently just out of reach. In a way, this mindset leads us to believe that life has truly begun once we've achieved our final goal, often overlooking the fact that life is happening right now, in every moment we spend focused on the future.

For example, we might tell ourselves that true happiness will come when we've saved a specific amount of money, bought a dream home, or achieved a certain level of professional success. However, once we reach these goals, they often bring only fleeting satisfaction before new ambitions and desires take their place. Without realizing it, we become so used to postponing that even when we're in a position to enjoy life, our minds are already looking to the next milestone. The present slips away unnoticed because we're perpetually living for an imagined future.

THE ASSUMPTIONS OF THE X AND Y DATES

This mindset assumes a degree of control over our lives that we don't have. In imagining a future "date X," where we will finally feel free to enjoy life, we behave as if we know precisely when the end, "date Y," will arrive. We act as though we can foresee how many years we'll have to enjoy our achievements, thinking that we'll know the perfect time to start living in the way we've always dreamed. However, the unpredictability of life doesn't allow for such assumptions. Dates X and Y are constructs, milestones we imagine in order to justify our present sacrifices.

The Chronopath, if it existed, would serve as a powerful reminder of the uncertainty of life. Showing us the time left would challenge the very concept of "someday" by confronting us with the finite nature of our lives. It would expose the arbitrary nature of these milestones, breaking down the illusion that we have all the time in the world to start living. With the awareness of time's brevity, we'd be reminded that the future isn't promised, and perhaps we'd be moved to bring our dreams forward rather than letting them live in the distant "someday."

LIVING FULLY WITHOUT WAITING

The illusion of "someday" can be dangerous because it subtly robs us of our present moments. By deferring our dreams and pleasures, we unintentionally tell ourselves that the present isn't good enough and that our lives are only worth living once we've met certain criteria. But true fulfillment isn't something to be stockpiled for later; it's something to be experienced now. It's easy to overlook the fact that we're always in the process of becoming, and every day brings opportunities to experience joy, satisfaction, and connection.

If we genuinely absorbed the wisdom that time is fleeting, we'd realize that every moment carries its own value. Rather than constantly striving for an endpoint, we'd focus on the quality of our current experiences, finding ways to appreciate and engage in our lives just as they are. This doesn't mean that we shouldn't have goals or strive for self-improvement, but rather that we shouldn't let these ambitions eclipse our present satisfaction. By focusing too much on "someday," we risk missing the beauty and richness of life as it unfolds.

THE ROLE OF THE CHRONOPATH IN BREAKING THE CYCLE

The Chronopath concept serves as a tool to combat this illusion by bringing our attention back to the here and now. Imagine glancing at your wrist to see not just the time of day but a reminder of how finite our lives are. It would urge us to ask ourselves, "What am I postponing? Why am I waiting for some imaginary future to feel fulfilled?" The Chronopath would be a powerful reminder to act in the present, to find joy and purpose without relying on distant milestones. It would encourage us to look at our lives more honestly, helping us to assess whether we're living in a way that aligns with our true desires and values.

For many, this realization could be a turning point, a call to examine what's truly important. If we're honest with ourselves, we might find that many of the goals we set for "someday" are fueled by societal expectations or external pressures rather than our own intrinsic motivations. The Chronopath would help us clarify what genuinely matters, inviting us to make room for these things in our lives right now instead of waiting for an undefined future. It would be a gentle but firm push to live in alignment with our inner compass rather than following an endless road of external benchmarks.

RECLAIMING LIFE'S SIMPLE PLEASURES

One of the most profound lessons in letting go of "someday" thinking is rediscovering the joy in life's simple pleasures. When we stop deferring happiness, we begin to see beauty and fulfillment in the everyday. A walk in nature, a shared meal with loved ones, a moment of quiet reflection—these experiences hold a value that doesn't require us to wait until we've reached a particular milestone. By appreciating these moments, we start to experience life in a more profound and satisfying way.

Imagine a life where we no longer view these small joys as "breaks" from the pursuit of bigger goals but as integral parts of a meaningful existence. Without the pressure of future deadlines, we become free to savor each experience fully. By letting go of the "someday" mentality, we reclaim our lives from the relentless pursuit of future satisfaction and begin to see that fulfillment is available to us right now.

EMBRACING A MINDSET OF PRESENCE AND PURPOSE

Breaking free from the illusion of "someday" means adopting a mindset of presence and purpose. Rather than seeing life as a race to some distant destination, we start to see each day as an opportunity to live authentically. It's about finding satisfaction in the journey rather than waiting for the finish line. The Chronopath symbolizes this shift, serving as a guide to remind us of life's impermanence and the importance of living fully in each moment.

In embracing this mindset, we learn that the future isn't a place where happiness resides; it's a projection of our hopes and dreams that will never materialize if we don't act on them in the present. The Chronopath wouldn't show us the end date to frighten us; rather, it would be a gentle nudge to savor the time we have, to pursue our dreams without delay, and to find meaning in the here and now. It challenges the illusion of "someday" by reminding us that our lives are happening right now and that waiting to live fully is a choice we no longer need to make.

By rejecting the idea of "someday," we embrace a life filled with presence, purpose, and gratitude. By focusing on today rather than deferring to tomorrow, we unlock the ability to live in alignment with our true selves, experiencing each moment for what it is—precious, fleeting, and profoundly meaningful.

WHEN LIFE FORCES US TO STOP

We're often jolted out of our routines by significant life events—unexpected and frequently unsettling. These moments, unplanned yet powerful, force us to pause and confront the reality of our existence, serving as sharp reminders of our eventual Y date. For me, that moment came during a terrible car accident. Late at night, I hit a tree and somehow emerged with my life intact. I was in my 30s, still energetic and ambitious, and within a month, I'd returned to my usual life, forgetting that brush with mortality.

Looking back now, I realize that the accident should have been my trigger to reflect. It was a moment that could have brought X and Y into sharp focus, urging me to make decisions with the awareness that time is limited. Instead, I brushed it aside, swept along by the current of life. If I could go back, I'd ask myself a crucial question: how would you live differently, knowing that time was limited? While I'm satisfied with many decisions I made in my youth, I realize now that acknowledging my eventual Y date could have helped me live more fully in the moment, savoring each phase of life.

Moments like this can serve as powerful reminders that our time is precious. They don't necessarily mean we need to overhaul our lives but rather recalibrate, to keep in mind that life is finite. They urge us to embrace moments of joy, struggle, and everything in between.

THE CONCEPT OF X AND Y DATES

The *Chronopath* watch idea comes to life through the notion of X and Y dates. In an ideal world where we knew both, we could chart a precise course, planning when to start, stop, and savor life fully. But without knowing our Y date, X becomes a moving target, a hazy goal we pursue without realizing that every moment spent working for a hypothetical future is a moment spent away from the present.

In our reality, we can't pinpoint when the end will come. Our Y date remains unknowable, and as a result, the X date —when we finally "arrive" and can relax—also fades into uncertainty. This ambiguity leads us to an endless cycle of postponing absolute joy as we endlessly strive toward an ill-defined goal.

If we truly understood that our Y date is unknown, we might focus less on the distant future and more on the now. We might find meaning in the small, everyday moments, recognizing that they're just as vital as any grand achievement. This perspective shift—living as if today were just as significant as some distant goal—could alter everything.

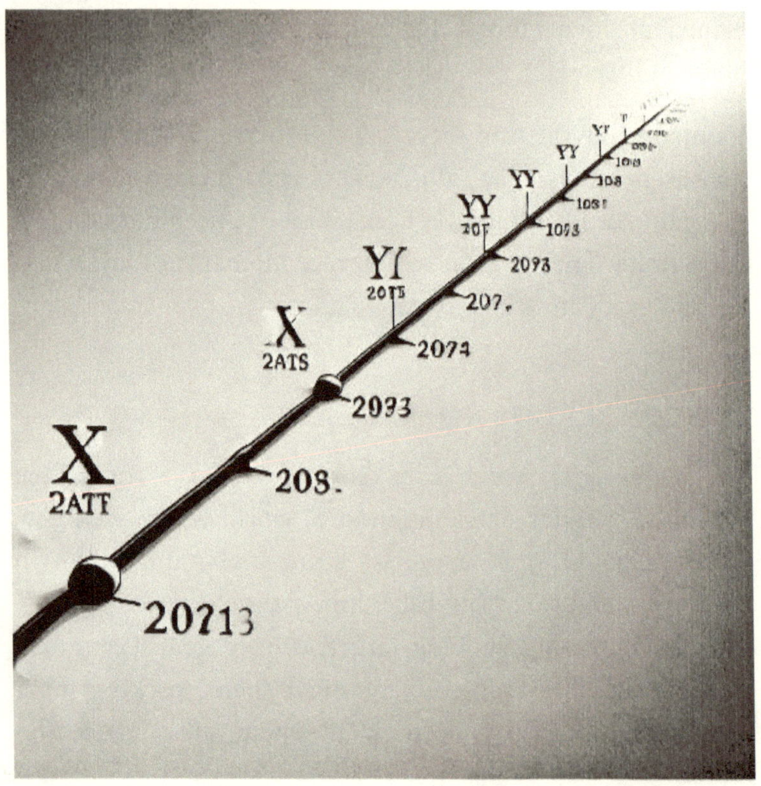

LESSONS FROM THE UNFORESEEN

As we move through life, we encounter moments that force us to reassess. Sometimes, we're confronted by our mortality or are reminded of the unpredictability of life. These moments often serve as catalysts, prompting us to consider what we'd do if we truly knew our Y date.

For me, it wasn't just the accident; other experiences—financial hardships, unexpected setbacks, and moments of failure—made me question the meaning of it all. During those times, I'd think about my Y date, asking myself, "If today were it, would I be proud of how I spent my life?" This thought process helped me see that my purpose isn't to reach some distant goal but to live meaningfully in each moment, whatever challenges or triumphs come my way.

These life events have a profound impact on how we view the passage of time and our sense of purpose. They remind us that it's okay to pause, to recalibrate, and to decide if our actions align with our values. Living with an awareness of the Y date is not about dread; it's about ensuring we're on a path that feels right.

EMBRACING THE Y DATE AS MOTIVATION

The notion of knowing our "Y date"—the hypothetical end of our journey—may initially sound unsettling, even morbid. But when approached with the proper perspective, it transforms into an empowering concept that sharpens our focus and helps us appreciate the life we have. Imagine knowing your time is finite, with a set endpoint. How would you live if each day brought you closer to a definitive date? If we could see the end, the certainty of our remaining time would push us to embrace experiences, nurture relationships, and pursue our passions with a heightened sense of value. Whether Y is tomorrow or a decade away, what matters most is how we choose to live and how we make each day count.

REDEFINING PURPOSE THROUGH THE Y DATE

Thinking about the Y date doesn't mean fixating on death. Instead, it can serve as a powerful reminder of life's impermanence, helping us to prioritize and make choices aligned with our true desires. By bringing this end date into view, we gain clarity on what genuinely matters. We're no longer bound by trivial pursuits, as each decision is filtered through the lens of purpose and fulfillment. Rather than being a dark thought, the Y date becomes a guiding force, one that encourages us to take risks, say the things we mean and live with authenticity.

Reflecting on the end doesn't strip life of its joy. On the contrary, it highlights the moments that bring true contentment and shows us how to spend our energy wisely. For example, I've found myself reevaluating my goals and daily choices, asking whether they contribute to my personal growth and happiness or are merely filling time. Embracing the Y date as a motivator shifts my focus away from what I "should" do, drawing me toward what truly fulfills me. In this sense, the Y date isn't a deadline; it's a tool for living fully and intentionally.

THE Y DATE AS A CATALYST FOR GRATITUDE

Acknowledging the Y date can be a powerful catalyst for gratitude. When we understand that our time is limited, the mundane takes on new significance. Simple pleasures—a conversation with a friend, a sunset, a meal shared with loved ones—are no longer just ordinary moments. They become treasures, opportunities to experience life's richness in the here and now. With each moment carrying weight and meaning, we begin to see that life isn't only about major achievements or future plans but is equally defined by the small, daily joys we often overlook.

Gratitude also softens our perspective on the difficulties we face. Challenges, losses, and even setbacks become part of the broader story, each contributing to our personal growth and resilience. Rather than dwelling on what didn't go our way, the Y date reminds us that these are part of our limited time. When we accept that time is finite, we're more inclined to forgive, let go of grudges, and move on from regrets. In the presence of the Y date, gratitude becomes a natural response to life's fleeting nature.

TRANSFORMING FEAR OF MORTALITY INTO PURPOSE

It's natural to feel some fear when we think about the Y date. Mortality is one of the most profound aspects of human existence, and the uncertainty around it can make us anxious. But, instead of allowing this awareness to paralyze us, we can transform it into a driving force for purpose. Viewing our mortality as a motivation to live well brings us closer to our core desires. Instead of hiding from the reality of the Y date, we can embrace it as a reminder that our lives have a beginning and an end—an arc that compels us to shape a meaningful middle.

Fear of the end can be replaced with a sense of urgency to live without regret. For example, by understanding that our days are numbered, we're more likely to pursue passions we've set aside, reconnect with people we've lost touch with, and speak our minds without hesitation. The fear becomes less about death itself and more about missing out on what matters most. When we use this awareness to fuel our decisions, we find ourselves living more authentically and purposefully, refusing to let opportunities slip by.

HOW THE Y DATE GUIDES DAILY CHOICES

Having the Y date in sight doesn't mean spending every moment contemplating our mortality. Instead, it acts as a subtle reminder to align our choices with our long-term values and aspirations. Each day becomes a chance to check in with ourselves: Are we spending time on what brings us joy? Are we nurturing relationships that enrich our lives? Are we dedicating energy to work that feels meaningful? The Y date provides a framework for evaluating these questions with honesty and intention, helping us stay grounded and mindful of how we invest our time.

For instance, rather than putting off dreams for a vague "someday," the Y date nudges us to act now. If there's a place we've always wanted to visit, a skill we've longed to learn, or a person we need to reconcile with, the Y date tells us not to wait. The presence of the Y date prompts us to embrace a bias toward action. In this way, every decision, big or small, becomes a step toward living with fewer regrets and a greater sense of fulfillment.

EMBRACING A LIFE WITHOUT THE ILLUSION OF FOREVER

One of the most significant benefits of keeping the Y date in mind is the dissolution of the illusion that we have forever. We're conditioned to believe that time stretches endlessly before us, and as a result, we may delay things that truly matter. However, when we recognize that life is finite, we see that each day is unique and irreplaceable. The Y date clears away the fog of complacency, making it easier to choose wisely and live without taking time for granted.

In this new perspective, we're able to appreciate life's impermanence as a gift. It's not about being somber but about being fully awake to each moment, with an understanding that our time here is limited. This shift encourages us to let go of fears that might otherwise hold us back—fears of failure, rejection, or judgment. Knowing that life doesn't last forever, we're more likely to pursue our goals, savor our relationships, and engage with life in a way that feels deeply meaningful.

LIVING EACH DAY WITH A SENSE OF COMPLETION

By embracing the Y date, we cultivate a mindset of living each day as if it were a miniature lifetime. Each morning becomes a fresh start, an opportunity to add value, seek joy, and create memories. This doesn't mean we won't have bad days or face challenges, but it changes how we approach each experience. When we see each day as potentially one of our last, we're inspired to approach it with gratitude, kindness, and resilience.

Living each day with a sense of completion isn't about perfection. It's about asking ourselves if, at the end of each day, we'd feel content with how we spent our time. Did we express love? Did we pursue something meaningful? Did we find a moment of joy, no matter how small? When we live with this sense of presence, we move through life without accumulating regret, knowing that we've made the most of each precious day.

CONCLUSION: THE Y DATE AS A PATHWAY TO AUTHENTICITY

Ultimately, embracing the Y date is about living with authenticity. It's a way to strip away pretenses and focus on what truly resonates with us at our core. When we acknowledge the limits of our time, we're encouraged to live in alignment with our values, without being distracted by society's definitions of success or happiness. This process of living authentically may involve letting go of old ambitions, redefining what success means, or simply being more present in our daily lives.

The Y date, though hypothetical, is a profound reminder of the life we want to lead. By keeping it in sight, we create a life filled with meaning, one that we can look back on with satisfaction, knowing that we lived fully and in tune with our true selves. In this way, the Y date isn't a final deadline but a continual invitation to live boldly, compassionately, and purposefully in each moment.

FINDING MY PURPOSE

In the midst of these reflections, I've come to recognize the importance of purpose. Stopping everything—pausing the relentless drive for achievement—has allowed me to look inward. I'm asking myself now: what do I truly want? What do I enjoy? Beyond financial success, beyond accolades, what brings me real joy?

Answering these questions means taking stock of what gives my life meaning. Supporting my family has always been a priority, but beyond that, I'm thinking about my passions. What would I pursue if I knew my time was short? Knowing that I am not someone who could be idle or disengaged, I'm searching for ways to fill my days with purpose, to build a legacy rooted in fulfillment rather than mere accomplishments.

LIVING WITH THE CHRONOPATH MINDSET

As I integrate the Chronopath mindset into my daily life, I remind myself that each day is a gift. I no longer need an exact Y date because I've chosen to live as though that date is just around the corner. This perspective has granted me freedom, allowing me to focus on what matters most without getting trapped in endless future planning.

I'm learning to appreciate small victories, simple joys, and the satisfaction of aligning my actions with my values. By approaching life with a sense of urgency—not anxiety—I'm choosing to prioritize experiences, relationships, and passions that resonate deeply.

LESSONS FOR THE FUTURE

Looking ahead, I see this journey not as a destination but as a series of choices that shape the person I am becoming. Each day, I strive to make decisions that bring me closer to my true purpose, knowing that the journey itself holds meaning.

The final lesson I leave with is simple yet profound: live today as though the Y date were a certainty. Fill each day with purpose, and find joy in the journey, not just the destination. The Chronopath watch, imaginary as it may be, serves as a reminder that life is finite. In each remaining moment, I aim to live fully, authentically, and with a profound appreciation for the time that remains.

Sharing the Lessons of The Chronopath

Too many of us are driven by fear, and if there's one thing that I hope this book will do, it's to help more people break away from this and live their life with trust and gratitude. Help me to reach more people with this message by taking a few minutes to leave a short review.

Simply by sharing your honest opinion of this book and a little about your experience of reading it, you'll make it easier for new readers to find it and reflect on how they can make their own lives more fulfilling.

Thank you so much for your support. We're on this earth for a short time, and we all deserve to live a life that truly fulfills us.

>>> **Scan the QR code below to leave your review on Amazon.**

FINAL CONCLUSION: EMBRACING THE JOURNEY AS IT IS

As I reflect on the path I've taken, a central moral emerges, one that is both simple and profound: by looking closely at where I am today and retracing each step that brought me here, I see that my life—its highs, lows, successes, and mistakes—unfolded precisely as it was meant to. Every decision I made, even those that felt challenging or uncertain, led to a future that felt uniquely right for me. Imagining other possible paths reveals how different my life might have been, but I now understand that each step and choice guided me to where I needed to be. In this way, my journey has led me to a place of acceptance, peace, and gratitude for the life I've lived.

The tool of reflection, embodied by my imagined concept of *The Chronopath*, became pivotal in this process. This hypothetical watch allowed me to imagine glimpses into the future, revealing potential paths while encouraging me to ponder the purpose of each choice. Yet, as I've come to understand, this journey isn't about trying to see or control what lies ahead. Rather, it's about learning to trust in the process, accepting the unknowns, and finding meaning in the experiences, relationships, and moments that fill each day. The lessons I've learned from each chapter of this journey have solidified this understanding, shaping my perspective on life's uncertainties, joys, and the wisdom gained from simply letting life unfold.

A FOUNDATION BUILT ON CHILDHOOD LESSONS

In the first chapter of my life, I explored the roots of my values, aspirations, and understanding of the world. Childhood is where we absorb the early lessons that guide us, even if we don't recognize their impact at the time. For me, these formative years were about building the foundation of my character—learning resilience, curiosity, and the importance of kindness.

Looking back, I can see how my experiences as a child shaped not only my personal values but also my approach to life. Childhood taught me to be open, wonder about the world, and carry that sense of wonder into adulthood. Through those early lessons, I learned that each moment has something to teach us and that true fulfillment begins with an openness to learning. This chapter reminds me that life's foundation is built not from grand achievements but from small, impactful experiences that resonate throughout our lives.

THE IMPORTANCE OF LETTING GO

In this chapter, I learned the profound value of flexibility. Life doesn't always follow a predictable path, and sometimes, the more we try to control our future, the further we veer from true fulfillment. One of the most memorable lessons I learned came from a golf game—an experience that taught me how important it is to ease up, avoid forcing things, and be adaptable.

Life's challenges and setbacks are often opportunities to practice resilience, embrace the unknown, and trust that things will work out, even if we can't see how just yet. As I reflect on this, I understand that flexibility is about more than adapting to change; it's about being open to possibilities and allowing life to unfold naturally. This mindset helps us find strength and peace, guiding us to adapt without compromising who we are or what we value.

TIME AS A PRECIOUS, FLEETING RESOURCE

In Chapter 3, I explored the concept of time, realizing that life's hours, days, and years pass swiftly. The days blend together, sometimes slipping by unnoticed. Reflecting on how quickly time has flown, I've come to appreciate its fleeting nature, knowing now that time spent is gone forever, making each moment invaluable.

If I had truly understood the value of time earlier, I might have approached life differently, but I now see that learning to cherish each moment is essential. The Chronopath watch became a metaphorical tool to underscore the importance of prioritizing time wisely, highlighting the necessity of living with purpose. Time is finite, but within that constraint lies the motivation to live meaningfully. Knowing that every moment counts pushes us to be more intentional with our time, prompting us to live fully and with gratitude.

OVERCOMING THE ILLUSION OF "SOMEDAY"

A common mental trap is the belief that happiness and fulfillment can be postponed to a future "someday." This mindset, however, often delays genuine contentment. In Chapter 4, I realized that deferring joy in the pursuit of achievements leaves us constantly seeking, never fully appreciating, the present. The idea that happiness lies in the future keeps us running on an endless treadmill, striving for milestones rather than enjoying life's moments as they come.

Reflecting on this illusion taught me to value each day and avoid waiting for some arbitrary point to begin living fully. Life is happening now, not at a vague "someday" that may never arrive. Realizing this, I've learned to find contentment in the present, embracing a mindset that appreciates today rather than waiting for an uncertain tomorrow.

EMBRACING THE Y DATE AS MOTIVATION

While the idea of having a "Y date"—a hypothetical endpoint —may seem grim, it actually transformed my outlook. Embracing our mortality can serve as a source of empowerment, motivating us to prioritize experiences, relationships, and passions. When we acknowledge that life has a finite span, we become more focused on what truly matters.

This chapter taught me that the Y date is not something to fear but a guiding reminder to live meaningfully, appreciate each day, and cherish those around us. Instead of fearing the end, I now see it as a reason to embrace life wholeheartedly without the burden of regrets. The Y date doesn't restrict us; rather, it inspires us to make the most of each day and build a legacy of joy, kindness, and purpose.

LESSONS LEARNED: EMBRACING THE JOURNEY

The culmination of these lessons has left me with a deep sense of gratitude. In life, it's easy to dwell on disappointments, to count our setbacks rather than our blessings. But as I've learned to reframe my experiences through a lens of appreciation, I realize that gratitude has transformed me. When we focus on what we have, our perspective shifts from scarcity to abundance, from dissatisfaction to fulfillment.

Gratitude has given me strength and resilience, allowing me to see each event as part of the journey and each experience as a building block. As I practice gratitude for even the smallest things—a warm sunrise, a quiet moment, a loved one's smile—I find that life feels fuller, more meaningful. This shift in focus has helped me trust that each choice, each experience, has its own place, guiding me toward a life that feels complete.

EMBRACING TODAY, LETTING GO OF TOMORROW'S WORRIES

Through this journey, I've come to realize that I no longer need to know every detail of what lies ahead. The desire to predict or control the future fades when we understand the richness of each present moment. If I knew everything about my future, life would lose its spontaneity and the joy of discovery. Embracing life as an unfolding adventure, I now feel that each day holds the promise of surprise, growth, and wonder.

Rather than seeking certainty, I've learned to live with a sense of openness. This outlook has allowed me to take on life with a lighter heart, to find beauty in each moment, and to appreciate the journey without fixating on the destination.

SHARING GRATITUDE WITH OTHERS

As I have come to appreciate what I have, I see how gratitude extends beyond my own life to touch those around me. Living with gratitude cultivates patience, understanding, and compassion. By choosing to appreciate what I have, I find more kindness in my interactions, and this positivity flows into my relationships. When we approach others with gratitude, we build bonds of trust and empathy, creating an atmosphere of generosity that enriches everyone involved.

Gratitude's impact on my life has shown me that sharing appreciation with others brings a profound sense of joy. It reminds me that life is more than just our own achievements; it's about the connections we create, the lives we touch, and the kindness we give and receive. With this perspective, my life is not just a personal journey but part of a larger tapestry of shared experiences and connections.

MOVING FORWARD WITH TRUST AND GRATITUDE

In the end, my journey with *The Chronopath* has taught me that life's essence lies in accepting the unknown, trusting in our choices, and embracing each day as it comes. We cannot control every outcome, but we can control our response to the path we're on. This realization has given me a sense of calm, knowing that I don't need to see every twist and turn ahead.

Living with trust and gratitude, I no longer worry about what lies around each corner. Instead, I take each step with confidence, knowing that I've built a life rich in meaning, one day at a time. My life may be filled with uncertainties but also with the lessons, relationships, and joys I have chosen to embrace. This journey has shown me that no matter the outcome, I am right where I am meant to be and that each step I've taken has been a vital part of the path.

THE FINAL LESSON: LIVING IN THE MOMENT

Ultimately, *The Chronopath* taught me that life isn't about controlling the future; it's about finding joy in the present and trusting in the journey. Life unfolds as it should, and each experience, both the triumphs and the challenges, serves a purpose. This journey has led me to a place of peace where I can look back on my life with gratitude and look forward with an open heart.

To everyone reading this, I hope my journey encourages you to reflect on your own path, to find gratitude in each moment, and to move forward not with fear but with trust. Our lives are the sum of the choices we make, the people we love, and the moments we cherish. Embrace them, for they are the true wealth of life.

REFERENCES

"TOP 25 LAST DAY QUOTES (of 223)." A-Z Quotes. Accessed November 14, 2024. https://www.azquotes.com/quotes/topics/last-day.html.

www.ingramcontent.com/pod-product-compliance
Lightning Source LLC
Chambersburg PA
CBHW031346060726
47590CB00007B/2641